Inspiring

WRiTiNG

in Primary Schools

Inspiring
WRITING
in Primary Schools

LIZ CHAMBERLAIN
WITH CONTRIBUTIONS FROM
EMMA KERRIGAN-DRAPER

AN
IDEA

Learning Matters
An imprint of SAGE Publications Ltd
1 Oliver's Yard
55 City Road
London EC1Y 1SP

SAGE Publications Inc.
2455 Teller Road
Thousand Oaks, California 91320

SAGE Publications India Pvt Ltd
B 1/I 1 Mohan Cooperative Industrial Area
Mathura Road
New Delhi 110 044

SAGE Publications Asia-Pacific Pte Ltd
3 Church Street
#10–04 Samsung Hub
Singapore 049483

Editor: Amy Thornton
Development editor: Geoff Barker
Production editor: Chris Marke
Marketing manager: Lorna Patkai
Cover design: Wendy Scott and Emily Harper
Typeset by: C&M Digitals (P) Ltd, Chennai, India
Printed and bound by CPI Group (UK) Ltd,
Croydon, CR0 4YY

The author and publisher wish to thank Emily Harper
for granting permission to use her artwork in the
form of the icons used throughout the text, and on
the cover.

Library of Congress Control Number: 2015959702

British Library Cataloguing in Publication Data

A catalogue record for this book is available from the
British Library

ISBN 978-1-4739-1610-4 (pbk)
ISBN 978-1-4739-1609-8

At SAGE we take sustainability seriously. Most of our products are printed in the UK using FSC papers and boards.
When we print overseas we ensure sustainable papers are used as measured by the PREPS grading system.
We undertake an annual audit to monitor our sustainability.

Contents

The authors

Liz Chamberlain is a Senior Lecturer in Primary Education at the Open University and is a former primary teacher, leading literacy teacher and Assistant Headteacher. Her main area of expertise is linked to the field of English and, in particular, children's home writing practices. Her interests focus on the ways in which children are positioned, and position themselves, as writers both at home and in school. She continues to work with children as co-researchers through the capture of on-going writing practices through the use of video and photographs. For four years she was the Strategic Consultant for the *Everybody Writes* national writing project and continues to use this work to reflect on effective literacy practices. She regularly runs after-school writing clubs in local schools.

Having been a teacher for almost 20 years, **Emma Kerrigan-Draper** is currently a headteacher in a small city primary school. Her main area of expertise is in mentoring and coaching teachers, both in her own school and across the authority, to improve teachers' practice, especially in the field of English. Prior to being a headteacher, Emma was an Advanced Skills Teacher with a focus on Primary English. She has a passion for using high-quality children's literature to inspire and motivate teachers to plan exciting lessons, which fuels children's appetites for reading and writing.

Acknowledgements

So many teachers and students have inspired this book. Teachers continue to ask about ways to inspire young writers in their classes, while students brought back new and creative ideas from school and reminded us of the importance of keeping writing on everyone's agenda. In turn, we have been inspired by Teresa Cremin, Prue Goodwin, Eve Bearne and Debra Myhill, who have all written extensively on the importance of audience, purpose, form, and the fact that any act of writing is an act of creativity.

Our thanks go to Tess Lowden, Abbie Hayter and Laura Simpson for their generosity in sharing their lesson plans for the history and technology chapters. Claire Williams is a young teacher of extraordinary talent and inspiring children to achieve their best in writing is at the heart of every lesson she plans and teaches. She and Vickie Peterson have both been happy to give feedback on the progress of the book and their comments were gratefully received and acted upon. Thanks go to Julie Wharton for ensuring the voices of those for whom writing presents additional challenges have been included. Darren Alderton from Grange Infants School provided some wonderful images of his classroom, and thanks also to Chris Brooks-Martin and the children at Hurstbourne Tarrant Primary School, and to Cupernham Infant School.

Emily Harper inspired the chapter on story writing based on her story stones lesson plans. Despite our dreadful descriptions, she managed to devise wonderful images, which appear throughout the book and an inspiring front cover.

Emma's voice, as a practising headteacher, is heard throughout this book, as is her message that all teachers need to adopt creative approaches to the teaching of writing, underpinned by excellent subject knowledge.

As the beginning of this book will highlight, listening to the voices of children as developing young writers is crucial for all teachers, and we have been lucky enough to watch and learn from Sid, Emily, Esther, Jack, Siobhan, Dylan, Lucia, Daniel, Johnny, Dominic, Jonas (and Emma), George, Millie and Sam. However, they won't thank us when they're older and we pull out the numerous scrapbooks we've kept of their thank you cards, get well soon letters, and random annotated drawings.

Foreword

by Teresa Cremin

What counts as writing?

What counts as writing in school? What should count as writing? Who defines this? Who has the right to define it?

As educated professionals teachers should surely be in the driving seat. They are responsible for framing what it means to be a writer in their classrooms and in best practice contexts they do so responsively. When teachers find out about their children's writing practices beyond the school gates, they tend to take a broader view of writing and of writers. If they are also aware of their own practices and preferences as writers, they are likely to be more sensitive to children's identities as young writers, and to recognise writing as an important form of identity work (Cremin and Myhill 2012). Young people, like adults, write to communicate, to make meaning, to sustain and negotiate relationships and to get things done. In the process they portray themselves in specific ways. As Ryan (2014: 130) observes 'writing is a social performance', a way of both exploring and enacting one's identity, whether in a text message, a Facebook entry, a diary or any other mode or medium.

Research suggests that from the earliest years, young children's writing interests and identities as writers are shaped by influential others, including their parents, peers and teachers (Dyson, 2009; Rowe, 2008). In particular, teachers' conceptions of writing and their classroom practice frame and mould the identity positions offered to young writers in school (Bourne, 2002; Bernstein, 2014). However in exploring what primary teachers understand composition to be, Yeo (2007) found that their conceptualisations were not connected to what they had been taught during teacher education, nor to the kinds of composition and literacy that operate in the 21st century. Rather their conceptions reflected their own childhood experiences of writing, and significantly their later 'induction into school literacy and classroom composition', which was very specific in nature and clearly influenced by wider policy contexts (Yeo, 2007:125).

Teachers are under pressure to ensure the young achieve the highest possible standards in national 'writing' assessments and this can (and often does) constrain what counts as writing in the classroom. In the last decade, the accountability agenda and the high profile afforded the apparent 'basics' in writing have created a considerable degree of compliance and conformity on the part of the profession, both in England and elsewhere. We have all seen teachers 'delivering' decontextualised stand-alone SPAG sessions (Spelling, Punctuation and Grammar); parcelling up aspects of grammar that are introduced, practiced and reinforced without reference to an author's intentions or to the audience, purpose or meaning of the text. Handing out greasy black and white worksheets downloaded from dubious commercial sites, which require the young to underline the modal verbs, conjunctions or adverbial phrases, does nothing to engage young writers. Furthermore, as research evidence demonstrates unequivocally, such practice is ineffective; there is no transfer of the skills 'taught' in this way to other contexts (Jones, Myhill and Bailey, 2012).

Yet the schooled version of writing is so persistently repeated and reinforced through curriculum requirements, assessment, training and teaching materials that it can become 'the norm', an almost unrecognised norm that is 'delivered' to young writers in order to help them reach 'the expected standard' of the day. This can seriously limit children's development as writers and restrict their opportunities to engage in meaningful writing in the real world. A balanced approach is needed to ensure that young writers develop the skills they need *and* the desire to write, and that they are supported in taking risks as writers, and use writing to make sense of their lives and their learning.

That is where this book comes in. Packed with accessible advice, engaging examples of research-informed practice and new ideas for ways to involve and support young writers, it offers primary teachers a breath of fresh air. Emerging from the memorable work of BookTrust's *Everybody Writes* initiative, which was co-led by Liz Chamberlain, and drawing on her own doctoral research, which involved exploring three young writers' practices at home and at school, the resultant mix of practice and theory - theory and practice is very energising. The authors take a real world view of writing and recognise and respect each child as a writer and each teacher as a professional – a potentially creative pedagogue.

Fully cognisant of the structures and strictures of the national curriculum and assessment, the authors offer teachers ways forward that are both engaging and evidenced as successful. The children's voices as writers and as learners ring out loud and clear, attesting to the passion and playful engagement of their teachers who make creative use of drama, storytelling, literature and multiple media to inspire them. Significantly the work is not confined to English, but draws on rich practice right across the curriculum. Examples from science, history and geography show how to integrate writing in meaningful ways that also link to literature and children's lives and interests beyond school.

The principles of teaching writing effectively are innovatively shared and use is made of engaging new metaphors to support young writers on their journeys. Liz Chamberlain, as lead author, recognises the need for children to unpack their backpacks of practice shaped by life experience, offers teachers a number of tools for navigating ways forward and highlights the significance of the destination. In the process both authors prompt us to reconsider writing and what counts as writing and challenge us to remain open to the ways this will shift over time.

References

Bernstein, (2014) Three planes of practice: Examining intersections of reading identity and pedagogy, *English Teaching: Practice & Critique* 13(3): 110–129.

Bourne, J. (2002) Oh what will miss say! Constructing texts and identities in the discursive processes of classroom writing, *Language and Education*, 16(4): 241–259.

Cremin, T. and Myhill, D. (2012) *Writing Voices: Creating Communities of Writers.* London: Routledge.

Dyson, A. (2009) Writing in Childhood Worlds. *The SAGE Handbook of Writing Development.* London: SAGE, 232–245.

Jones, S. M., Myhill, D. A., and Bailey, T.C. (2012). Grammar for writing? An investigation into the effect of contextualised grammar teaching on student writing. *Reading and Writing*, 26(8), 1241–1263.

Ryan, M., and Barton, G. (2014). The spatialized practices of teaching writing in elementary schools: Diverse students shaping discoursal selves. *Research in the Teaching of English*, 48(3), 303–328.

Rowe, D.W. (2008) The social construction of intentionality: Two-year-olds' and adults' participation at a preschool writing center. *Research in the Teaching of English*, 42(4): 387–434.

Yeo, M. (2007) New literacies, alternative texts: teachers' conceptualisations of composition and literacy, *English Teaching: Practice and Critique*, 6 (1): 113–131.

Introduction

Key words

Mastery, purpose, audience, choice, creativity, engagement, motivation, developing confident and flexible writers.

Tools for inspiring writing

The aim of this book is to provide a practical and useful resource for teachers with ideas that might be likened to tools for inspiring writing. The book hopes to provide a theoretical basis for understanding and articulating pedagogy in a way that is accessible, yet challenging for teachers. The aspiration for the book is that it finds its way into the hands of student teachers, but also into the hands of the early career teacher as well as the more experienced old hand. The underlying principle of the book is that teachers need to be confident teachers of writing, as much as they need to be writing teachers. They need to write, as Eve Bearne insists, *in the presence of their classes* (2002:30) and while for some teachers this presents a challenge, for others it provides an opportunity to share what they love about the writing process.

Writing does things to people: it makes them anxious, excited, concerned, confused or even appreciative of a time and space to reflect and transform thoughts into text. Reading has the same effect, but to a lesser degree, and this is mostly because for much of the time it is easy to appear to be a reader. Go to the library, pop a book under your arm and during quiet reading or ERIC, open it up and stare at the letters on the page. No one really knows that reading is a struggle, or that the words appear mixed up or can even guess that the sheer effort of decoding the words leads to a burden on the cognitive load. However, with writing it is all too clear that you find it tricky. The second the pen hits the page your secret is out: the way you form your letters, your choice of vocabulary or the empty white page broadcasts to anyone passing your table that writing for you is hard. You can see the good writers. Their heads are down, their ideas appear to be flowing and they can probably spell and have the neatest of handwriting. Maybe you recognise yourself in those two descriptions and maybe that was how you felt as a child, or even as an adult. The point is a simple one. You will meet those two writers in your classrooms and every possible combination in between. You have to plan for them, motivate them, enthuse them, plan their learning against the national curriculum, assess them and explain them as developing and improving writers. This book aims to provide you with a framework for being successful in both teaching writing and talking about it, both in the initial chapters which focus on the theoretical elements of writing and the subsequent more practical chapters based on writing sessions that will inspire quality written outcomes.

The book is divided into two main sections:

What it means to be a developing writer – an overview of writing research, including attitudes and perceptions framed within the national curriculum;

Creating spaces and places for writing – an exploration of the opportunities for writing within subjects, other than English. Exemplar planning is presented for writing across subjects and through out-of-school projects that may bridge the gap across home and school.

What it means to be a developing writer

The first four chapters provide an overview of what it means to be a developing writer both in and out of school. That, coupled with the way in which writing is defined, is reflected in the attitudes of teachers and children. Chapters 1 and 2 challenge the reader to reflect on their own pedagogy and to consider the messages communicated to children through the ways in which writing is framed in their own classes. In addition, the importance of writing conversations and the need for text-rich classrooms will be championed as effective ways in nurturing developing writers.

Chapter 3 encourages the reader to look beyond their current practice by seeking out additional writing opportunities. Recent research into teachers as readers and writers highlights the importance of early career teachers becoming the role models for readers and writers in their own classrooms. Embedded throughout this section will be a focus on the drivers which determine the book choices we make and the impact these have on the children in our classes. In addition, the aims and purpose for writing, as laid out in the national curriculum (DfE, 2013), will be unpicked together with a discussion of how teachers need to adapt their current pedagogy in order to embrace the shift in focus. The emphasis will be on supporting students and teachers in preparing and teaching writing that supports the growth of flexible writers; those who are able to adapt to a range of writing scenarios fuelled by a rich foundation of spoken language, quality texts and experiences.

Creating places and spaces for writing at home and at school

In Chapters 5 to 10, there is a focus on reflecting the previously discussed pedagogy for writing through practical suggestions as to what writing activities might look like in your classroom. The exemplars in Chapters 5 and 6 are based on subjects that will be familiar to you in the primary curriculum: history and geography. They have been chosen to illustrate how particular subjects offer the writer a chance to practise particular elements of writing and are supported by a teacher's toolkit for writing. For example, in geography the bridge between narrative descriptions and visual representations is suggested through the use of specific and technical vocabulary, while in history the emphasis is at word level through time-related connectives and the use of a chronological framework. However, these examples should always be viewed as a snapshot of what writing might typically look like in your classroom, rather than being taken out of context as a one-off lesson.

Having challenged the reader to think about writing within subjects, the exemplars in the next four chapters illustrate how different experiences can motivate and enthuse young writers. In order to do this, a range of stimuli will be suggested, including using storytelling, drama, children's literature and poetry as starting points, which hopefully all feel like familiar good practice. However, also included are examples that use popular culture and technology as key components in inspiring young writers. In each of the chapters, children's writing examples are included to illustrate how purposeful writing activities can and do lead to high quality written outcomes.

The final two chapters of the book consider the places and spaces for writing beyond classroom walls and into the home. Two innovative approaches to writing within the community are explored: Writers Workshop and the use of a Storysack©. These approaches have a long history in primary classrooms but they have been chosen to best represent the ways in which the shared spaces they offer can form a writing bridge between home and school.

An interactive experience

This book also practises what it preaches in promoting the fact that reading, writing and speaking and listening are interdependent, as we know *reading and writing float on a sea of talk* (Britton, 1983:11). Therefore, as you read, look out for the four different tasks required of you as the reader: Over to you, No Excuses, Jottings and Ta Dah!. These tasks may require you to reflect, to discuss, to write, to record, to think, or to practise, but all require you to challenge your thinking and consider making changes to your practice.

OVER TO YOU

Take an idea and make it your own.

NO EXCUSES

These are the non-negotiables of your classroom.

JOTTINGS

Something for you to write or record to capture first thoughts, or to reflect on.

TA DAH!

A piece of child's work or a comment designed to illustrate or demonstrate the point being discussed.

Exploring the world that is writing

You may have noticed that the front cover of this book suggests that developing writers need to be explorers and pioneers setting out on a journey that explores the new world of writing. Writing provides possibilities, and this is a recurrent theme throughout the book. With your pen or pencil or even with a keyboard, you can make things happen, find your voice and communicate. The aim of writing is to connect; your words may reach out to an audience, known or otherwise, through diary entries or creative words strategically placed on a page. Writing can also transform how you think; you may have experienced rereading something you've written and been surprised at its fluency or clarity. We also know, through what published authors tell us (Cremin and Myhill, 2015), that writing pushes at the boundaries; the writer navigates through unknown territories ready to follow new plotlines, or discovers a symbiotic relationship between a piece of text and an illustration or that through the pattern and order of a few simple words they have created poetry that stops the reader in her tracks.

The book suggests that the children we teach are travellers across the writing process; they travel across home and school and build on and develop their familiar and newly-learned practices (Chamberlain, 2015). Across this exploration they develop new and transformative writing practices (Dyson, 2008) and create cultural bridges across home experiences into an imagined life mirrored in school writing lessons. In particular, the book suggests that as children embark on their writing expedition to becoming confident and flexible writers, they develop a mastery over their writing that can be likened to the creation of a backpack of practice, where skills and practices are selected dependent on the task.

References

Bearne E (2002) *Making Progress in Writing*. London: RoutledgeFalmer.

Chamberlain, L (2015) *Exploring the out-of-school writing practices of three children aged 9–10 years old and how these practices travel across and within the domains of home and school,* Educational Doctorate thesis, The Open University.

Cremin, T and Myhill, D (2015) Professional writers' identities and composing practices, *Symposium presentation at UKLA: Re-assessing literacy: Talking, Reading and Writing in the 21st Century,* 10–12 July, Nottingham, UKLA.

Dyson, AH (2008) Staying in the (Curricular) Lines: Practice Constraints and Possibilities in Childhood Writing. *Written Communication*, 25(1): 119–159.

1 Children and writing

Introduction

> *Writing is among the greatest inventions, perhaps the greatest invention, since it made history possible.*
>
> (Robinson, 2009:7)

The most fascinating thing in the history of writing is that, although it has been a tool used for over 6,000 years, it is only in the last 150 years that writing has been a skill within reach of most of the population. The first writing systems were based on pictures and hieroglyphs before they moved into alphabets and syllabic structures that matched sounds and syllables with corresponding letters and shapes. Writing also originally concerned money, with a primary function to record financial transactions, so it feels rather disappointing that its roots are not more connected with creativity or self-discovery. Some of its other functions included predicting the future or the setting down in writing of laws and decrees, for which archaeologists and historians are grateful, as this was the key to understanding early writing systems. It was the discovery of the Rosetta Stone in the early nineteenth century that led to a modern understanding and subsequent translation of Ancient Egyptian hieroglyphs, a system far more sophisticated and complex than merely pictures representing words or ideas. The Stone was written by a group of priests in three languages: Greek (the language of the rulers), hieroglyphic (used for official Egyptian documents) and demotic (the common script of the day) and it listed all the good things that the pharaoh Ptolemy V had achieved for the people. The fact that it was written in three languages is a testament to the power of text – by ensuring as wide an audience as possible would allow for as many people as possible to read the good words of the priests and the good deeds of the pharaoh.

It took many more centuries for writing to travel to Europe and even longer for the invention of paper to revolutionise people's access to writing. In the 1870s, when education in England became government-financed, children were taught to read and write. Together with the Industrial Revolution, this led to writing becoming more widespread. Prior to this, while some of the population could be considered 'literate', the definition at the time meant only being able to read and comprehend, with most available reading material centring on biblical scriptures. Writing also belonged to those in the privileged classes, as it was they who had access to the necessary tools, like pens and paper. It was earlier, back in the fifteenth century, that Johannes Gutenberg invented interchangeable, reusable print, leading to the drop in prices of printed materials, such as books and newspapers. The printing press was also responsible for some of the problems with our English writing system. A Flemish printer working for William Caxton (who brought the printing press to England and is credited with standardising the English language) decided that 'ghost' should have an 'h', as that was how it was spelled in his language. David Crystal (2013) argues that knowing these stories behind our often incomprehensible spelling system makes the language come alive – the added benefit is to make awkward spellings easier to remember.

Fast forward five centuries, and advancements in technology mean that whether through our text messages, status updates, blogs or tweets, being able to write means being able to participate. These foundations are laid in classrooms up and down the country, where the inspiration for a positive relationship with writing can be sparked. Therefore, this book aims to demonstrate how writing can be exciting, whilst still meeting the requirements of government policy and national curriculum statements. It will also stress the importance of confident and skilful teachers with excellent subject knowledge for English, providing children with real reasons for writing, which in turn will enable them to become enthusiastic and developing young writers. Some of the ideas in the book will be familiar, and this is deliberate. The book aims to show how the exemplar activities can be adapted and refined rather than through the presentation of a set of stand-alone sessions. Most importantly, this is a book about children as writers: examples of children's writing will be used throughout to exemplify or illustrate points of interest. As is appropriate, all the young authors gave permission for their work to be used and, therefore, their writing is not to be judged or assessed, rather it provides a picture of what is possible.

Early writers

From an early age, children want to write. They try their hardest to let the grown-ups know that their print carries meaning until, finally, we can decode their messages. Children in Reception classes role-play writing and use what they learn in school to transform home-writing experiences. Here, three-year-old Jonas demonstrates his new-found writing ability and declares to his mum that he has 'written' his name.

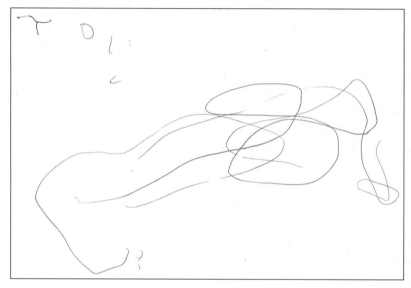

Figure 1.1 Jonas's map

At first, your eyes might be drawn more to the map that illustrates the journey of the pencil around the page. However, look at the top left-hand corner and you can just make out some letters; there's an attempt at a 'J', certainly an 'O' and maybe at the end you can see a sideways 'N'.

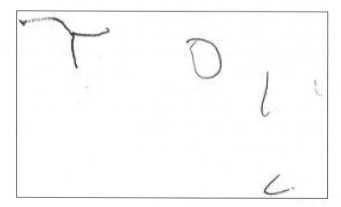

Figure 1.2 Jonas's name

Jonas is demonstrating what Marie Clay (2000) would describe as an understanding of concepts about print, in that he is writing from left to right, each individual letter is clearly demarcated and there is an attempt at a capital letter. Most importantly, just as the example you see below, he understands that print carries meaning.

These very young children are participating in writing activities, both at school and in the home, which allows them to borrow and revise their early mark making and whilst these initial experiences may have been shaped by the adults or copied from siblings, it is the children themselves who *contribute to the maintenance and transformation of these practices* (Gazkins *et al.*, 1992, as cited in Dyson, 2009).

TA DAH!

For example, in her homework, four-year-old Maisha demonstrates her difficulty in writing the word 'chicken' on a worksheet – all too familiar to Reception class teachers.

Figure 1.3 Chicken worksheet

However, two weeks later, and at home, Maisha writes the sentence *Chickens can lay eggs*, all by herself.

Figure 1.4 Chickens can lay eggs

As readers, we will never know if she knew that the word *chicken* defeated her the first time and that since then, and behind the scenes, she has been practising getting it right. What is clear, however, from her new sentence is that she can not only now spell the tricky word: Maisha has moved on from the understanding of individual letters making up words, and her words have now become sentences that make sense and carry meaning.

How children learn to write

The theory of how children learn to write and, furthermore, how they become successful writers remains under-researched, when compared with research into reading (Myhill, 2005; Kress, 1994). One key theorist was Vygotsky (1982): his work at the beginning of the twentieth century highlighted that children discover through the process of learning to draw things that they are beginning to draw speech. This in turn becomes a method of writing letters and words and very soon they begin to realise that reading and writing does something, it communicates and it has a purpose (Vygotsky, 1982:117). His notion was that as written language develops, it becomes a complex and new form of speech; a system that allows meanings to be attached to signs and symbols. This in turn leads to a blurring of what constitutes a writing activity. For example, reflect back on Jonas's map – was this a piece of writing or was he drawing? A study by Larkin (2010) into early marking-making found that young children do not register a difference between these activities because both involve using a pencil. So in a sense, when children learn to write they are *'learning to represent aspects of their world'* (Parr *et al.*, 2009) and, therefore, in order to shape their texts, children need to draw on their personal interpretations of the world and events. As you review a child's piece of writing you are reflecting on their complex social worlds where *'already existent texts intermingle to create new ones'*. This may be presented in a multimodal format including texts combined with oral, visual or gestural modes

(Christie, 2003:288). This notion of a combination of images and text colliding to create new meanings is illustrated in six-year-old Ben's Christmas writing.

Jottings

Read through Ben's writing and make a list of all the features that he's included, remembering to reflect back on Christie's notion of multimodal writing (2003).

Figure 1.5 Ben's Christmas writing

What did you have on your list? Maybe you thought about context and started your list with *It's Christmas*, perhaps you thought about the surface features of his writing and included *Knows about apostrophes*, or possibly *Writes from left to right*. All of which are correct, but what is invisible to the reader is the 'where' and 'when' of this piece of writing. It is an artefact that captures a particular point in time.

What the reader is unaware of is that six-year-old Ben is attending his granddad's funeral, surrounded by busy adults doing the kinds of things that adults do at funerals. Ben sits at the kitchen table with the stickers and pens given to him by his grandma and he crafts his text. His work does what Christmas messages should do: it offers a bit of hope, is interactive and multimodal, and just as with a song or poem, it invites the audience to listen. The writing also demonstrates something deeper than the text on the page: it helped him to connect an unfamiliar situation with something familiar. That is the power of writing. It allows children to put into words and pictures how they feel.

Demands on the young writer

Cremin and Myhill (2012) argue that writing is a deliberate act and one that has to be taught – shaping thoughts into words is complex. Writing is also not a 'one-off' activity, hence the emphasis this book places on writing as a process, or a layered experience – one that builds on previous experiences and, hopefully, leads to more crafted and refined writing. In the 1980s and 1990s the notion of writing as a *verb*, rather than as a *noun*, was emphasised (Bearne, 2002). The idea was that the process of writing is just as important as the output or product. If, like Vygotsky, we make the connection between speech and writing, it makes sense to reflect on the process of writing words with that of the spoken word. Speech is fleeting and relies on a shared experience. The speaker is encouraged by a listener who supports, extends or just nods in acknowledgement at what the speaker is saying. Writing can be transitory. It might be a note or a typed word that is quickly deleted or rubbed out, but it is more often precise and organised. Writing requires ideas and needs time to be crafted, and as the words come together on a page or screen, a permanent record of those ideas or thoughts is created. This is what can make writing so challenging for young writers. If you are aware that you cannot spell well, or if you know that your handwriting is tricky to read, this can make the act of writing feel like a daunting prospect. For the developing writer in your classroom, these things matter, as will be further discussed in Chapter 2.

Over to you

Think about the writing that you have done over the past week and make a list. Having created the list, think about the types of writing you completed and for what purpose. Was the writing an end in itself, or did the writing contribute to a different type of end product? If you had a shopping list, then the end product would have been a cupboard full of food. If there was a note to a family member, then maybe there was the conveyance of an emotion or an instruction.

Further reflection on what is on your list of writing will also give you an insight – not only into your own definition of writing, but also the extent of your writing. You may have found yourself surprised by the amount, or indeed the lack of writing you created. Furthermore, did your list include emails or text messages? If so, your view of writing may reflect the more recent, and previously mentioned, multimodal approaches to text design. Were there any examples of handwritten letters or cards to family members who would not have appreciated a more digital form of communication? All of these things are important when you are designing authentic and appropriate writing activities for your classes.

Over 30 years ago, Frank Smith (1982) suggested that in order to understand the complexities and challenges of writing, it helped to separate it into two specific areas: transcriptional skills and compositional skills. Composition skills are concerned with getting ideas, the grammar and selection of words – in essence, doing what authors do – and the transcriptional skills involve the physical effort of writing, including the spelling, capitalisation, punctuation, paragraphing and legibility of the writing (Smith, 1982:20). You may also see these terms referred to as authorship or secretarial skills (Latham, 2002) and what is being suggested is that writers bring together ideas *about* a piece of writing – *the compositional skills* – and skills *for* the writing – *the transcriptional skills*. While it may be obvious that in order to write, you need to have something to write about and the skills to write it down, Smith went further and argued that in order to be a successful writer, the compositional and transcriptional skills should be taught separately – and that transcriptional skills should always be last (1982:23). This is an interesting parallel, as is discussed in Chapter 3, to the presentation of the national curriculum for writing (DfE, 2013) where transcription, which includes grammar, handwriting and spelling are presented first. It is for you to decide if you think this is a deliberate positioning of transcription as being more important than composition, or ideas for writing. Note also the shift from Smith's (1982) use of grammar for composition to a narrower concept of grammar for structure and organisation.

Individual voices

All children in your class will benefit from a range of approaches to composition and transcription skills, and this is particularly true of children who may have cognitive problems, for example dyslexia or dyspraxia. Such children may find these dual demands of writing difficult. In order to support them, consider the differentiation and personalisation of their writing tasks. It is important to lay the foundations for writing with an emphasis on oral work, and for composition, look for alternative ways for children to record their ideas. Children who have sensory impairments will benefit from writing tasks that are adapted to their specific needs – and this may involve having a multisensory approach or using other adults as scaffolds, or who can remove the barriers that transcription skills can present. The use of visual cues and symbols can support those children who have social and communication difficulties with the chance to share their ideas with a focus on content rather than on the handwriting or spelling. But for all children, providing a purpose for writing needs to be at the core of quality writing experiences, and this is what should remain at the heart of your practice, regardless of government changes and policy initiatives.

Policy and practice

Over the last 50 years, the teaching of writing has been typified by very public debates about concerns over writing attainment (Ofsted, 2009; Fisher, 2006; Ofsted, 2005). In addition, discourse has been characterised by a concern over teachers who do not teach writing well, first highlighted in the 1980s White Paper *Teaching Quality* (DfES, 1983). At this time, practice in England was strongly influenced by approaches to writing instruction emanating from the US and Australia, which led to the introduction of the over-prescriptive National Literacy Strategy (DfES, 1999). For over 30 years, the teaching of writing has focused on particular models of classroom writing: the workshop approach (Graves, 1983); the skills-based approach (Berninger and Swanson, 1994); genre theory (Snyder, 2008) and, more recently, through a return to a skills-based approach within a prescriptive curriculum (DfE, 2006) which has now metamorphosed into the same skills-based approach, but within a less prescriptive but more accountable framework (DfE, 2013).

Government policy rarely mirrors the type of engagement with writing that happens for children away from their classrooms, and therefore it fails to recognise how teachers might build on the type of writing that children are doing at home. This is reflected in Ofsted reports (2009; 2011) which suggest that schools make insufficient links with children's out-of-school experiences and, consequently, children feel that English is a subject with little relevance to their lives.

Where does that leave the knowledge that Emily demonstrates in this story written at home?

As a Year 2 pupil, Emily might not be expected to create such a lengthy text as this, or to use phrases such as 'soft and sound', rather than the expected *safe and sound*. Or indeed, maybe a

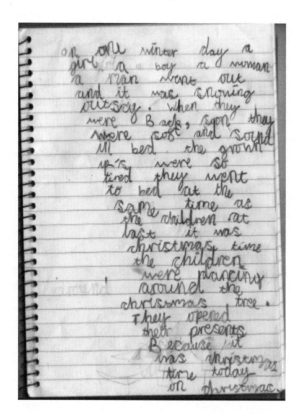

Figure 1.6 Emily's story

target for her would be to make sure the writing began at the margin. However, what she is telling the reader is that she likes writing and that she is enjoying telling a story based on her real-life Christmas experience. She may also be writing more at home than at school, so where is the opportunity in Emily's classroom for her to share these out-of-school practices?

No excuses

Ensure that your classroom is a place where children have the time and space to write.

In addition, drop the drawbridge between home and school and invite children to bring in and share their home-produced writing, or find out what skills or techniques they bring to a new piece of writing.

At the heart of the writing process is the notion that meaning-making is of huge importance for children and their teachers, who need to plan writing activities that are engaging and meaningful. When children know that the writing does matter, they write more and they write better. Bearne (2002) asks practitioners to question whether they are writing teachers, or teachers of writing, and this is a question that this book will continue to refer back to.

If we want children to write enthusiastically and creatively, then teachers need to have that same enthusiasm when it is time to start writing. One of the features of high-quality literacy lessons is when teachers have good subject knowledge and a clear understanding of the individual needs of their pupils (Ofsted, 2009:53). As a writing teacher you need to have considered some of the wider debates about writing. For example, you may already have very specific views about the nature of English as a subject (Ofsted, 2009:19), or you may have a particular attitude towards writing. Beyond the practical considerations in planning writing, what is crucial is the extent to which you are aware of your role in supporting the young writers in your classes. Therefore, the starting point is to know what children think about writing and whether your definition of writing matches theirs.

References

Bearne, E (2002) *Making Progress in Writing*. London: RoutledgeFalmer.

Berninger, V and Swanson, H (1994) Modifying Hayes and Flower's Model of Skilled Writing, in Butterfield, E (ed.) *Children's Writing: Towards a Process Theory of Development of Skilled Writing*. Greenwich, CT: JAI Press.

Britton, J (1983) Writing and the Story of the World, in Kroll, B M and Wells, C G (eds) *Explorations in the Development of Writing: Theory, Research, and Practice*. New York, NY: Wiley.

Christie, F (2003) Writing the World, in Hall, N, Larson, J and Marsh, J (eds) *Handbook of Early Childhood Literacy*. London: SAGE.

Clay, MM (2000) *Concepts about Print: What have Children Learned about Printed Language?* Portsmouth, NH: Heinemann.

Cremin, T and Myhill, D (2012) *Writing Voices: Creating Communities of Writers*. London: Routledge.

Crystal, D (2013) *Spell It Out*. London: Profile Books.

DfE (2013) *National Curriculum in England: Primary Curriculum*. London: DfE.

DfES (1983) *Teaching Quality*. London: DfES.

DfES (1999) *National Literacy Strategy*. London: DfES.

DfES (2006) *Primary National Strategies – a framework for literacy*, London: DfES.

Dyson, AH (2009) Writing in Childhood Worlds, in Beard, R, Myhill, D, Riley, J, *et al* (eds), *The SAGE Handbook of Writing Development*, pp.232–245. London: SAGE.

Fisher, R (2006) Whose Writing is it Anyway?, *Cambridge Journal of Education*, 36(2): 193–206.

Graves, DH (1983) *Writing: Children and Teachers at Work*. London: Heinemann Educational Books.

Kress, G (1994) *Learning to Write*. Abingdon: Routledge.

Larkin, S (2010) *Metacognition in Young Children*. Abingdon: Routledge.

Latham, D (2002) *How Children Learn to Write: Supporting and Developing Children's Writing in School*. London: PCP.

Myhill, D (2005) Ways of Knowing: Writing with Grammar in Mind, *English Teaching: Practice and Critique*, 4(3): 77–96.

Ofsted (2005) *English 2000–2005: A Review of Inspection Evidence*. London: Ofsted.

Ofsted (2009) *English at the Crossroads*. London: Ofsted.

Ofsted (2011) *Excellence in English*. London: Ofsted.

Parr, J, Jesson, R and McNaughton, S (2009) Agency and Platform: The Relationships between Talk and Writing, in Beard, R, Myhill, D and Nystrand, M (eds), *The SAGE Handbook of Writing Development*, pp.246–259. London: SAGE.

Robinson, A (2009) *The Story of Writing*. London: Thames & Hudson Ltd.

Rojas-Drummond, S. M., Albarrán, C. D. and Littleton, K. S. (2008) Collaboration, creativity and the co-construction of oral and written texts, *Thinking Skills and Creativity*, 3 (3): 177–191.

Scheuer, N, de la Cruz, M, Pozo, JI, Echenique, M and Marquez, MS (2009) Kindergarten and Primary School Children's Implicit Theories of Learning to Write, *Research Papers in Education*, 24(3): 265–285.

Smith, F (1982) *Writing and the Writer*. London: Heinemann.

Snyder, I (2008) *The Literacy Wars*. Sydney, Australia: Allen & Unwin.

Vygotsky, LS (1982) *Thought and Language*. Cambridge, MA: MIT Press.

2 Sharing definitions of writing

Introduction

This chapter will discuss – in what will become a familiar feature of this book – the fact that writing is not a subject. At some point, and embedded in pedagogical mythology, is the notion that writing lessons only take place in the morning because they need to be included in the pattern of a school day that requires concentration and effort. As teachers, we need to ask what message this gives to children about what writing is – and the role it plays in their lives. As discussed in Chapter 1, children write outside of school and – if the definition of writing is broadened – then they will tell you they enjoy writing. This has implications for you as a teacher. You may be disappointed if, when you ask your children to create a written response to an exciting input, you are expecting to see posters, mind maps, captions, pictures or annotated diagrams, but your class just stare at the blank piece of paper you put in front of them. They may anticipate that the writing outcome you desire has a specific genre and that it needs to fill the entire page because that is what previous teachers have expected of them. This is not the fault of the teachers – this is as a result of policy and the high-stakes testing culture in our schools that has put increasing pressure on written outputs being seen as evidence of learning, rather than as a creative or crafted act. However, you can shift this imbalance by ensuring that in your classroom you have shared your definition of writing with all the writers in the classroom... and that includes you.

Chapter 4 will introduce a pedagogy of writing and propose an approach to the writing process that is creative but also structured. Its aim is to support you as a writing teacher to understand all the ingredients that lead to quality writing. However, it is within this current chapter that the discussion focuses on children as writers, their perceptions of writing and, most importantly, what it is that makes the difference to them when it comes to writing lessons in their classrooms. Throughout the chapter, we will return to the idea that writing does not take place within a subject called English; writing is part of reading, of speaking, and of listening, and it is also the vehicle through which learning in other subjects can be communicated. Being a writer runs parallel to being a reader. You learn from other writers by being exposed to quality children's literature, and this means learning *to write like a reader and read like a writer*. As Margaret Meek reminds us,

> *To read is to think about meaning; to write is to make thinking visible as language. To do both is to become both the teller and the told in the dialogue of the imagination.* (1991:48)

Attitudes to writing

Lay three sticky notes in front of you. On each one complete the phrase *'Writing is…'* Write down your first thoughts before moving onto the second, and the third. If you have more ideas then record those as well. Try not to be academic or clever, just write down whatever comes into your mind. When you have finished, have a look at your impressions of writing. You might have written *'Writing is hard'*, or maybe *'Writing is about spelling or handwriting'*; sometimes students put *'Writing is creative'* or *'Writing is personal'*.

You can understand the aim of the task: reflecting on your own thoughts about writing, and this should lead you to start thinking about what writing will look like in your classroom. Ultimately, you are creating and crafting your own definition of what writing will look like in your classroom – and how you will support children in becoming accomplished writers.

Recent studies from the US and England would suggest that attitudes towards writing are shifting and with advances in technology there is a need to re-classify what might be included in a category headed *Writing*. In the US-based, PEW Internet study (Lenhart *et al.*, 2008), young people reported that they wrote a lot, with 93% saying that they wrote for pleasure but only if 'electronic' texts were included. However, 60% of the same young people did not actually consider electronic texts as writing (2008:2). The following year, a similar study by the National Literacy Trust (Clark and Dugdale, 2009) found that 75% of young people in England say that they write regularly (if the definition of writing includes writing text messages, posting on social networking sites or using instant messaging).

However, the important consequence of a more recent National Literacy Trust survey (Clark, 2015) is the apparent gender divide across pupils aged 8–16, with 19% of boys consistently saying that they do not enjoy writing compared with only 8% of girls. Of these, 18% of boys reported that they were *not very good* writers, compared to 13% of girls. In a separate study, children aged 7 were asked to write to a younger child explaining what they needed to know about writing in their class (Wray, 1995). What was striking in the research was that the most frequently mentioned aspects were spelling and neatness, with children also advising others not to make the writing too long in case the teacher got bored. This study is over 25 years old, but the National Literacy Trust survey in 2009 of 3,000 children and young people suggests that children still consider being a good writer involves primarily having good handwriting and the ability to spell (Clark and Dugdale, 2009). An action research project into raising boys' achievement in writing noted that it was those in middle primary classrooms who reported as having the most gains having been part of the project. The boys self-reporting to the question, 'Do you enjoy writing?' rose from 75% at the beginning to 100% by the end (UKLA, 2004). This, coupled with an increase in confidence and motivation, led to the boys holding more positive attitudes towards writing, which was then reflected in higher teacher assessments of their written work (UKLA, 2004). However, this contrasts with a study that took place across eight schools with children aged 8 to 10, who shared not only negative attitudes about writing, but also expressed their anxieties about writing (Grainger *et al.*, 2005). And what we know from research by Dunsmuir and Blatchford (2004) is that those who are anxious about writing say they do not enjoy it and have difficulty generating content. In addition, this research also suggests that teacher assessments of a child's attitude towards writing strongly relates to their actual writing attainment.

The seminal National Writing Project in the 1990s suggested that children's perceptions of *writers* is that they are the people who publish books (usually stories) while any act of writing is often thought about in terms of the end product (National Curriculum Council, 1990). So, there is work to be done to convince children that writing is a process; writing is creative and full of possibility.

Imagine being able to write about dragons, landing on strange planets, or imagining a different end to a familiar story. Consider the prospect of making any ordinary day suddenly extraordinary and all because you, as the teacher, chose a word or a sentence that turned you into an adventurer and your class into explorers. That's what writing can do.

Children's perceptions of themselves as writers

Research about children's perceptions of writing often relies on a teacher's knowledge about the kinds of writing children may take part in outside school. One such study of primary children's creative writing practices reported that 64 out of the 80 teachers interviewed were able to identify children in their classes who wrote regularly at home because of the writing artefacts they brought in from home (Brady, 2009). The responses were based on questionnaires and the teachers' *perceptions* of the types of writing and writers within their classes. For example, one teacher reported that 40% of her class wrote at home, while another reported that there were no children in his class who wrote at home. Within these classes *writing* was framed as 'creative' or 'imaginative'. However, it may be that some of the other types of multimodal writing the children engaged with at home were just not visible to the teachers, because the children kept their writing hidden. A small-scale case study of three middle-primary children (Chamberlain, 2015) uncovered the types of private or *sub-rosa* writing children engage with at home and which they choose to keep from adults. The research took place in the children's homes and in their classrooms where they were observed making decisions about the writing practices and artefacts they chose to share with adults at home and school. At home, the children had ownership over their writing, which was in contrast to the way they presented themselves as writers in school. At school they struggled to complete writing in the time frame and their teachers often described them as finding it difficult to generate ideas for writing. Therefore, only asking teachers about the writers in their classes – without understanding the children's *out-of-school* writing – may mean that some of the writing they engage with remains undiscovered and unvalued.

Another larger ethnographic study took place over a school year in a middle primary, multi-ethnic classroom (Bourne, 2002:241) and it found that children are positioned in classrooms according to the relative power they hold as so-called *competent* writers. Those considered good writers had regular conversations with the teacher about the content and detail of their writing, whereas those who were less successful engaged in teacher/pupil talk characterised by questioning that highlighted the children's mistakes in their writing.

However, by asking children about their favourite writing or asking what makes a good writer, teachers can gain valuable insights into what they think writing is for. Two groups of children in Year R and Year 4 were asked to reflect on why it was that their teachers said that they were good writers (Bearne *et al.*, 2011). The younger children were very clear about their role as listeners and how moving into good writing was marked by independence with them showing an awareness of some key ingredients for writing, as in the case of the child who referred to making 'stories and characters'. The older children have begun to identify the interplay of reading and writing and its impact on their development as writers in terms of being able to widen their vocabulary because of their rich reading experiences.

Reception	Year 4
Why do you think your teacher says you're a good writer?	
We write by ourselves. We write so beautifully. We write our own stories without any adults. We listen to the teacher about what we have to write. We have good writing. We make some stories and characters.	I'm going to be an author because I've got a good imagination. I'm a reader and a writer. I'm more of a reader than a writer. I never talk when I'm writing. I use strong adjectives like gigantic instead of big.

Table 2.1 Why do you think your teacher says you're a good writer?

Another key question asked was '*What does your teacher need to know about you and writing?*'. One poignant comment was from a Year 4 boy who said '*I like writing, even though I'm not very good at it*'. The message to his teacher was clear, '*even though I don't think I'm very good (and maybe you don't think I'm very good either), I still enjoy it*'. One girl wrote '*I never finish stories*' and when probed as to why that might be, it was not because she got bored, or didn't know what to write, it was quite the opposite. She had so many ideas for writing she moved from one idea to another too quickly while to her teacher it looked as if she never completed anything.

Therefore, it is unsurprising that children's definition of writing is often a reflection of their teacher's approach to writing. The classroom where writing is viewed as a dynamic and collaborative endeavour will be mirrored in the accomplished writers who are motivated and enthusiastic about their writing.

Writing conversations

How will you know what children in your classroom think about writing? It's quite simple – you need to ask them. Using a perceptions survey, or asking the same kinds of questions used by Bearne *et al*. (2011) are both good ways of finding out what children think about their writing. However, a simpler way is to start a conversation about writing. There are regular spots on the timetable for you to do this, most notably in guided writing sessions: giving you a weekly opportunity to talk to groups of children as they collect ideas, draft their writing or ask them about what they think of their writing. Myhill and Jones (2009) suggest that children should always have the opportunity to reflect on their writing by talking about the decisions made throughout the writing process and ultimately in the evaluation of their final draft.

This ongoing process, underpinned by talk, contributes to children developing as writers through the refinement of their writing. By ensuring that speaking and listening about writing is central, children can begin to articulate with all aspects of their writing, whether it is explaining a vocabulary choice or defending a plotline. As James Britton stresses, *reading and writing float on a sea of talk* (1970) and over 40 years later, this principle is reflected in the current national curriculum, *Spoken language underpins the development of reading and writing* (DfE, 2013:3). So maybe your response to whether writing is a product or process (Bearne, 2002) is that it has to be both. The quality of the product is ultimately influenced by the extent to which there has been a shared understanding and communication of the process between you as the teacher and the children as evolving writers.

In addition, Chamberlain (2015:205) proposes that teachers take on the role of 'souvenir hunters' by asking children to share favourite pieces of writing, which can often reveal the multiple understandings about the composition and purpose of the writing. This coupled with asking children to talk through their work provides a useful framework for understanding more about children's chosen writing practices, and it may also reveal what writing means to the children in your class.

Here, nine-year-old Milly's map is an example of a kept and favourite piece of writing that reveals how she perceives writing. You may argue that what you are looking at is a drawing not a piece of writing, but for Milly, maps are writing. They communicate ideas, and there is text in the form of labels and captions. Rather than a finished product, the map is the basis of a game. The map is part of a spy game that Milly plays with her friend and it involves two characters making their way around the island to find a hidden 'base'.

Figure 2.1 Milly's map

As you review this piece of writing, consider the additional information that Milly shares in a writing conversation. Milly has kept this artefact since she made it some years ago when she lived in Berlin. The fact that she chose to bring the map back with her to England reflects the important symbol the map has perhaps become. It represents a different time and place and reminds her of her early friendships which she wishes to retain and recall. All of this information could easily have remained hidden, so the importance of the map as a symbol of friendship would have been lost. The message is clear – talk to children about their writing and understand what motivates this type of personal response. For Milly as a writer, this kept artefact reveals her captured childhood memories of playing with old friends. Writing is so much more than just marks on the page defined by a teacher's learning objective.

 ## Attitudes to writing

Create your own writing conversation framework by gathering questions you might ask children about their writing. Here are some suggestions to get you started:

- Are you a good writer?

- Do you enjoy writing? Why?/Why not?

- Can you remember a piece of writing you did when you were younger that you were particularly proud of? Why was that?

- What's the best piece of writing you've done recently? What was good about it?

- Do you ever write/draw at home? What kinds of things?

- Does anyone else write/draw at home?

- What advice would you give someone younger than you to help them get better at writing?

A text-rich environment

If we want children to enjoy learning, then reading and writing need to be everywhere. It needs to be obvious to every child what topic they are learning through the wall and practical displays. Showcasing the importance of writing can be achieved through the displays and learning can be scaffolded with word walls that the children can refer to when writing, by displaying 'tricky' words as a reminder when spelling. Or choose a poem, write it out, put it up and let children respond (Rosen undated). Let children be explorers in their classroom and see it as a place where there is always something new to discover. Who wouldn't want to be a writer in this classroom where 'Exciting Writers' are at work?

Have a book of the week, nominate a child to bring in a favourite book from home and display it in a prominent place. Let the child explain why the book is important to them

Figure 2.2 Exciting writer at work

23

and allow other children to respond – before you know it, there will be a unique library of favourites.

The national curriculum highlights that, *Reading also feeds pupils' imagination and opens up a treasure-house of wonder and joy for curious young minds* (DfE, 2013: 4). Put reading for pleasure at the heart of your teaching by reading daily to your class (regardless of the year group), which will ensure that the children in your class have access to quality children's literature to share and enjoy together. There is also another more immediate impact on children's writing ability: those who are good comprehenders use their story knowledge to tell structurally coherent stories (Cain, 2003:348). The suggestion here is that by reading aloud, there is an additional benefit to children who find comprehension difficult to grasp when they read independently because of their over-focus on word reading. By listening to stories read aloud by a more experienced reader – you – they have the chance to improve their comprehension skills, which in turn supports them in getting better at telling stories, which then helps them become better comprehenders. In short, it is a virtuous circle. However, what is crucial is that the reading aloud of texts is not used as a tool for analysis, but instead the focus is simply to enjoy being read to and having the time and space to take on board the structural content of different genres.

In interacting with and reading quality texts, both fiction and non-fiction, children learn that the texts act as good teachers or models and can be used to support their own writing (as discussed in Chapter 4). Barrs and Cork (2001) refer to this as *the reader in the writer* while others maintain that children who know how texts work are more likely to be successful writers (Flynn and Stainthorp, 2006:61).

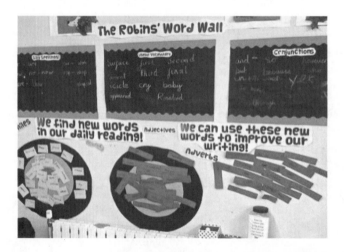

Figure 2.3 Robins' reading wall

In this classroom, the teacher has made the reading and writing links explicit for the children by challenging them to find new vocabulary in their reading and to find ways of using it in their writing. The children are being encouraged to play with words and meanings in a way that Grainger, Goouch and Lambirth (2005) propose makes confident and aspiring young writers.

A report by the National Literacy Trust (Clark and Poulton, 2011) suggests that children who have books of their own enjoy reading more than those who have limited access to books. Therefore, ensure your book corner is well stocked so that children have access to a range of reading material: quality literature, poetry, non-fiction, magazines, annuals or comics. This might encourage them to go home and share reading with their parents or they might visit the local library, which will in turn further support them as readers (Goodwin, 2010). Ask the children to help plan the book-corner, and let them decide on the theme and what to include: they might choose cushions, chairs, a listening station, boxes of books or a special entrance. You may wonder why you should spend time making your classroom comfortable for reading, but studies have shown that changing the physical environment of your classroom can promote the time that children spend with books (Morrow and Weinstein, 1986).

No excuses

There is no excuse for your classroom to be bereft of purposeful text and quality literature.

Audit your current classroom provision and consider what messages it gives the children about the value you place on reading and writing. Decide on one change you can make to improve it, and then act on it. Create an author exhibit, shadow a book award, create a classroom book, or celebrate different kinds of writing (yours included).

Writing which reflects real life

Daniel Pennac (2002) talks about the *The Rights of the Reader* and his freely available poster outlining all ten rights should have a celebrated spot in your reading corner. One of his suggested rights is *The right to mistake a book for real life*. Many of us will relate to this by recalling past reading experiences which may have surprised us with the uncanny ability to reflect our own experiences, almost as if the book must have been written for just us. Writing too can provide similar opportunities. The power of writing has already been discussed in terms of a child's ability to decide on any turn of events simply at the turn of a vocabulary or plotline decision. Research also suggests that children write about or engage with writing practices which reflect the significant events of their lives, or they write with or for people who are important to them (Chamberlain, 2015; Earl and Grainger, 2007). A research project into the reading and writing lives of 71 five-year-olds determined that the children wrote at home with a range of family members, as well as writing by themselves (Nutbrown and Hannon, 2003). Both these factors have implications for writing in your classroom: children like to write about events which they have direct experience of, and they enjoy writing with others.

Daniel Pennac (2002) further suggests such radical moves as *the right not to read* and *the right to read out loud*, which no teacher can argue with. However, where would *the right not to finish a book* or *the right to be quiet* fit in with the national curriculum (DfE, 2013) requirements of reading?

In 2011, a group of Buckinghamshire teachers working as part of a pilot project called 'Teachers as Writers', within the national writing project (NWP), discussed the notion of ten *Rights of the Writer*, which were then written and illustrated by Simon Wrigley. This mirrors Daniel Pennac's ten *Rights of the Reader* illustrated by Quentin Blake. According to the projects' founders and co-authors Wrigley and Smith (2010), The '*Rights*' were, in part, *an expression of the project's classroom approach, which gave young writers greater ownership of the writing process.*

1. The right not to share.

2. The right to change things and cross things out.

3. The right to write anywhere.

4. The right to a trusted audience.

5. The right to get lost in your writing and not know where you're going.

6. The right to throw things away.

7. The right to take time to think.

8. The right to borrow from other writers.

9. The right to experiment and break rules.

10. The right to work electronically, draw or use a pen and paper.

Again, some of the rights immediately feel like common sense, but what about those that raise more practical questions for you? For example, what about #6 *The right to throw things away?* What happens if that was the only piece of writing completed in the lesson and that writing was your only opportunity to assess that child's writing, or to demonstrate learning took place? It is worth taking a few moments to read those which feel comfortable, those which raise questions and those which you feel would be impossible in your classroom, or appear to challenge your pedagogy. Cremin and Myhill (2015) have further argued for a modification of Pennac's rights to parallel a set of rights for children as writers. What you realise when you ask children to do this is just how complicated the writing process is – and what children in your class have absorbed having been a writer in your class.

Year 6 Emily and Sid have created their own Ten Rights of the Writer. On first reading it is interesting to consider what they think is important and, on second reading it is interesting to consider the order of their ideas.

For Sid, writing is about others' ideas with built-in breaks with writing only happening when the moment 'hits' you. For Emily, spelling and punctuation are important. And, playing with the rules and taught grammar of writing are obvious targets for her rights. What is unclear from both children is how competent they are at writing and this is what is so powerful about asking children to create their rights. We are unsure whether Emily's insistence that

	Sid	Emily
1	The right to magpie from others.	I have the right to deliberately misspell words.
2	The right to have breaks.	I have the right to deliberately use punctuation incorrectly.
3	The right to write when the moment hits you.	I have the right to 'and' at the start of a sentence.
4	The right for it to sit in your room.	I have the right to write wherever I am.
5	The right to not let your parents see.	I have the right to write with a leaf.
6	The right to not be criticised.	I have the right to write whatever I want.
7	The right to not have your parents make suggestions.	I have the right to write an unrealistic story.
8	The right to have time to write.	I have the right to write about someone else's life.
9	The right to use whatever you want to write or type with.	I have the right to publish anything I want.
10	The right to write whatever you want.	I have the right to write lies.

Table 2.2 Ten Rights of the Writer (by Sid and Emily)

the transcriptional elements of writing are prioritised above *the right to write about whatever she wants*, is because spelling and punctuation are more difficult for her, or in fact that she is a capable and playful writer who wants to bend the conventional rules. Sid too reveals what is important for him: writing is personal and sometimes solitary and it needs the thoughtful editor rather than the perceived potential of what author Jeanne Willis refers to as the *harsh critic* in the form of other adults. What of Emily's right to write lies, or to write an unrealistic story? For teachers, there are two ways of viewing these ideas: either you see the possibility of creating problems in the primary classroom as the diversity of the young writers is revealed, or you relish the opportunity to find out more about the young writers and what might just make the difference to them when faced with a writing activity.

TA DAH!

Create ten Rights as a Writer for you as an adult. Consider how these might be different to how you are expecting children in your class to view writing. Ask the children to write their own, then display them and use them. Look for different ways of incorporating some of the children's ideas into your pedagogy for writing, establish shared definitions of writing and create a community of writers (Cremin and Myhill, 2012) where writing motivates developing writers through a collaborative process that is both authentic and meaningful to their lives.

References

Barrs, M (2004) The Reader in the Writer in Grainger, T (ed.) *The RoutledgeFalmer Reader in Language & Literacy*. London: RoutledgeFalmer.

Barrs, M and Cork, V (2001) *The Reader in the Writer*. London: CLPE.

Bearne, E (2002) *Making Progress in Writing*. London: RoutledgeFalmer.

Bearne, E, Chamberlain, L, Cremin, T and Mottram, M (2011) *Teaching Writing Effectively: Reviewing Practice*. Leicester: UKLA.

Bourne, J (2002) Oh, What Will Miss Say!: Constructing Texts and Identities in the Discursive Processes of Classroom Writing, *Language & Education,* 16(4): 241–259.

Brady, J (2009) Exploring Teachers Perceptions of Children's Imaginative Writing at Home, *English in Education,* 43(2): 129–148.

Britton, J (1970) *Language and Learning*. Oxford: Heinemann.

Cain, K. (2003) Text comprehension and its relation to coherence and cohesion in children's fictional narratives, *British Journal of Developmental Psychology*, 21: 335–351.

Chamberlain, L (2015) *Exploring the out-of-school writing practices of three children aged 9–10 years old and how these practices travel across and within the domains of home and school*, published thesis. Milton Keynes: The Open University.

Clark, C (2012) *Young People's Writing in 2011: Findings from the National Literacy Trust Annual Survey*. London: National Literacy Trust.

Clark, C (2015) *Young People's Writing in 2014: Findings from the National Literacy Trust Annual Survey*. London: National Literacy Trust.

Clark, C and Dugdale, G (2009) *Young People's Writing: Attitudes, Behaviour and the Role of Technology*. London: National Literacy Trust.

Clark, C and Poulton, L (2011) *Book Ownership and its Relation to Reading Enjoyment, Attitudes, Behaviour and Attainment.* London: National Literacy Trust.

Cremin, T and Myhill, D (2012) *Writing Voices: Creating Communities of Writers*. London: Routledge.

Cremin, T and Myhill, D (2015) Professional Writers' Identities and Composing Practices, *Symposium presentation at UKLA: Re-assessing literacy: Talking, Reading and Writing in the 21st Century,* 10–12 July. Swansea: UKLA.

Department for Children, Schools & Families (2006) *Primary Framework for Mathematics & Literacy*. London: HMSO.

Department for Education (2013) *English Programmes of Study: Key Stages 1 and 2. National Curriculum in English*. London: DfE.

Dunsmuir, S and Blatchford, P (2004) Predictors of Writing Competence in 4- to 7-year-old Children, *British Journal of Educational Psychology*, 74(3): 461–483.

Earl, J and Grainger, T (2007) I Love to Write at Home – There I'm Free, *Seminar presentation at UKLA: Thinking Voices,* 6–8 July. Swansea: UKLA.

Flynn, N and Stainthorp, R (2006) *The Learning and Teaching of Reading and Writing.* Bognor Regis: John Wiley & Sons Ltd.

Fox, R, Medwell, J, Poulson, L, and Wray, D (2001) *Teaching Literacy Effectively in the Primary School.* London: Routledge.

Goodwin, P (2010) *The Literate Classroom.* London: David Fulton.

Grainger, T, Goouch, K, and Lambirth, A (2005a) *Developing Voice and Verve in the Classroom.* Abingdon: Routledge.

Grainger, T, Goouch, K and Lambirth, A (2005b) Playing the game called writing: children's views and voices, *English in Education,* 37(2): 4–15.

Lenhart, A., Arafeh, S., Smith, A. and Rankin Macgill, A. (2008) *Writing, Technology & Teens,* Washington, US, Pew Internet.

Meek, M (1991) *On Being Literate.* The Bodley Head: London.

Morrow, LM and Weinstein, CS (1986) Encouraging voluntary reading: The impact of a literature program on children's use of library centres, *Reading Research Quarterly,* 21: 330–346.

Myhill, D. and Jones, S. (2009) How Talk Becomes Text: Investigating the Concept of Oral Rehearsal in Early Years' Classrooms, British Journal of Educational Studies, 57: 265–284.

National Curriculum Council (1990) *National Writing Project: Perceptions.* London: Nelson Thornes.

National Writing Project – Evidence, findings, recommendations and practical classroom approaches are freely available and can be found on the National Writing Project website: **nwp.org.uk** (accessed 15.1.16)

Nutbrown, C and Hannon, P (2003) Children's perspectives on family literacy: Methodological issues, findings and implications for practice, *Early Childhood Literacy,* 3(2): 115–145.

Ofsted (2009) *English at the Crossroads.* London: Ofsted.

Pennac, D (2006) *The Rights of the Reader.* London: Walker Books.

Rosen, M (undated) *The Poetry Friendly Classroom,* **www.michaelrosen.co.uk/poetryfriendly. html** (accessed 15.1.16)

Smith, F (1994) *Writing and the Writer.* Mahwah, NJ: Lawrence Erlbaum Associates.

UKLA/PNS (2004) *Raising Boys' Achievement in Writing.* Royston: United Kingdom Literacy Association.

Wray, D (1995) What do Children Think about Writing, *Educational Review,* 45(1): 67–77.

Wrigley, S and Smith, J (2010) Making Room for Writing, *English Drama Media,* 18, London, NATE.

3 Writing in the national curriculum

Introduction

In the years following the introduction of the National Literacy Strategy (DfES, 1999) there was a tendency to view writing as a predominantly skills-based process within a prescriptive literacy curriculum (Fisher, 2006). Some of these criticisms were answered with the Primary Framework for Literacy (PNS) (DfES, 2006). The PNS outlined the text types for non-fiction, fiction and poetry units of work that should be taught across both key stages. Planning exemplification was provided that promoted the inclusion of creative initiatives, such as the use of film shorts, drama and multimodal texts. The focus was very much on a text or genre-type approach to writing together with the focus on purposeful writing activities.

In the old Primary Framework (DfES, 2006), units of work were listed under specific genres: narrative (adventure, myths and legends, descriptive etc.), non-narrative (persuasive, explanatory, instructional etc.) and poetry (a variety of forms). As teachers became more familiar with the expectations of each unit, their approach became more flexible and it was common to see topics leading the teaching of specific units. For example, a topic on the *Environment* might start with an information unit reflected in fact-finding and research activities, which was then followed by a unit on persuasive writing through letter writing to the local Council requesting more recycling bins.

There was also a move to make the teaching of writing more explicit by providing a meta-language for writing. The original National Literacy Strategy (1998) introduced some useful terminology such as *word*, *sentence* and *text level* and *Grammar for Writing* (DfEE, 2000:152). It remains a useful document for newly-trained teachers as it outlines the organisation and language features of different text types. In understanding the linguistic structure of the different genres, teachers are able to go beyond a discussion about the transcriptional aspects of writing, the spelling, handwriting and punctuation, and to begin to talk about the required *writerly knowledge* (DfEE, 2000). The kind of knowledge needed to be successful in crafting successful writing, for example, talking about the content of the piece and how a different choice of vocabulary might lead to a different response for the reader. Myhill *et al.*'s (2013) work around teachers' grammatical knowledge of writing suggests that teachers often overuse the notion of *effectiveness* within the context of generic feedback to children about their writing. In particular, the research suggests there is a reliance on feedback focused on students improving their writing *for effect* (p.86). However, too often, teachers are not telling children the detail of next steps by suggesting a specific example to support the change, or how the change might improve or refine the writing.

Another influential project was *Raising Boys' Achievement in Writing* (UKLA/PNS, 2004) which promoted the need for teachers and children to provide sufficient time to journey with writing. The project also outlined a three-phase approach to writing:

Phase 1 – familiarisation with genre

Phase 2 – capturing ideas

Phase 3 – shared writing, guided writing into independent writing.

Teachers readily adopted the approach, and this practice, despite the introduction of a new national curriculum in 2014, is still evident in many classrooms. Projects including *How Talk Becomes Text* (Myhill and Jones, 2009) and *Talk for Writing* (DCSF, 2009) further emphasised the need to make talk an essential component of quality writing through the use of talk-based strategies such as drama and role-play activities. Fast forward to September 2014 and the roll-out of a new national curriculum for England and Wales and a time of yet more change for teachers in the planning of quality writing in their classrooms. For some teachers, the change has led to an undesirable and narrow conceptualisation of writing which fails to reflect the demands of an increasingly technological twenty-first century or to acknowledge the well-documented multimodal forms of writing that children engage with outside of school (Cremin and Myhill, 2012; Bearne and Wolstencroft, 2007). However, it does reflect the current high-stakes testing culture in schools (Cook-Gumperz, 2006; Fisher, 2006) and the need to assess writing outcomes in such a way that assumes the ability to monitor and compare across schools, while expecting uniformity across teachers' understanding and expectations.

National curriculum, 2014

In the national curriculum (DfE, 2013), the programme of study for writing is expressed as separate components: transcription, composition, vocabulary, grammar and punctuation. This also allows teachers to think more broadly about the purpose of the writing, rather than focus on one specific genre. This is a useful reconceptualisation of writing. Previously, teachers were beginning to grapple with the fact that writing does not always fit within a box called 'persuasion' that is always a non-fiction unit. Sometimes persuasion can be presented in the form of a poem or narrative; therefore, it is perhaps useful to think more broadly and incorporate a number of genres within a specific unit of work headed 'Purpose of the writing'. For example, if as part of a Year 4 topic on the Victorian seaside the aim of the English unit of work or short-term planning is 'to entertain', then children might write and tell their own musical hall jokes, compose a murder mystery set in an old hotel or even create instructions about how to make puppets in a Punch and Judy show. This approach also allows teachers to make immediate connections across all three aspects of English spoken language, reading and writing, and to make appropriate links that reflect their inter-relatedness.

What has been reflected in the most recent English curriculum is the division across transcription and composition. And, as already discussed when Frank Smith's work (1982) was being shared it is transcription that appears to lead the way.

Transcription comprises spelling and handwriting. **Composition** ideas are articulated and structured, as children work on planning, revising and evaluating their writing. Before being distracted by the specific requirements, statutory and non-statutory, allocated to each year or phase, it is crucial to digest the *Purpose of Study*. In this introduction we garner the aims of the teaching and the learning and get a sense of the wholeness of the learner as they move through their primary learning. Upon reading, there are clear themes that can be identified within both the Purpose of Study and the Programmes of Study for Spoken Language, Reading and Writing. In particular,

- **The importance of the Spoken Language in the development of the reader and the writer**

    o   Spoken language underpins the development of reading and writing. (2013:3)

- **The negative impact on learners who leave the education system unable to speak, read or write well**

    o   All the skills of language are essential to participating fully as a member of society; pupils, therefore, who do not learn to speak, read and write fluently and confidently are effectively disenfranchised. (2013:3)

- **The importance of being able to speak, read and write as the tools of communication**

    o   A high-quality education in English will teach pupils to write and speak fluently so that they can communicate their ideas and emotions to others and through their reading and listening, others can communicate with them. (2013:3)

- **Effective communication is underpinned by accuracy in the preciseness of our language (vocabulary) and technical language use (grammar)**

  o The National curriculum for English aims to ensure that all pupils acquire a wide vocabulary, an understanding of grammar and knowledge of linguistic conventions for reading, writing and spoken language. (2013:3)

As with any curriculum presented by any political party, the decisions taken are based on key drivers of the day and English and literacy will always be to some extent a political football. Currently, it is the PISA (OECD, 2012) rankings that dominate the direction that education departments globally turn to and a country's policy is changed in accordance with their apparent success (or otherwise) measured against reading test attainment outcomes of 15 year olds. This is not unique to the UK – if you look at any country not listed in the top 5 (currently Shanghai China, Singapore, Hong Kong China, Taiwan, Korea), you will see a country grappling with the ways in which it can improve the literacy outcomes for children and young people. The top European country, Liechtenstein, comes in at number 8, while the UK has risen two places on 2009 and comes in at number 23. At this point it is best to let you reflect on your sharp intake of breath.

Embedding knowledge and understanding learning

Within the new curriculum there has been a pedagogical shift – with a focus on 'facts' and its apparent requirement for children to *know* things. However, it also requires a more in-depth examination in the way that learning is set out for a particular year group or phase. The expectation is for learners to concentrate on developing a deep and truly embedded knowledge and understanding of their learning. The pedagogy requires teachers and children to learn, practise, experiment, apply and, finally, master new skills, which can only be truly grasped with the necessary and associative knowledge.

Therefore, an academic year might look like this:

Autumn Term	Spring Term	Summer Term
Learn skills	Use skills and apply them to a common context	Apply skills to a range of contexts and evidence mastery through choice

Table 3.1 Cascading of skills across the academic year

A model as simple as this presents a number of questions:

- How do we hook in and engage learners in what could be a very 'dry' learning environment in the Autumn term?

- How does a model like this look in Key Stage 2 when learning is organised over a two-year phase?

- How do teachers define the notion of 'mastery' within the context of the standards linked to performance descriptors?

From a headteacher's perspective, this creates challenges in the way that teaching looks across a school year. Many consider it to be reflected as a cyclic model of learning where teachers bring learners back to look at skills repeatedly. It is rather like learning to cook a basic recipe and then, upon returning to it, making refinements and improvements, eventually using it as the base for something different. Without those basic skills being truly embedded and understood, there can only ever be limited success of application and even then, it may not come with a conscious awareness of the learner, as opposed to an intuitive application.

The interdependency of reading, writing and spoken language

An oversight within the PNS (2006) was the lack of explicit reference to speaking and listening, and this led to the introduction of the now infamous *lunchbox* of 'Speaking, Listening and Learning materials', which opened up the debate about the role of talk in the classroom. The latest curriculum (DfE, 2013) refers to Spoken Language and embraces the key role that high-quality models play for children in broadening, deepening and enriching their vocabulary and encouraging accurate use of language. Rooting our writing in an understanding of purpose, and how it relates to our everyday spoken languages, makes a solid connection between how we really use language and why and how we commit oracy (the ability to express oneself fluently/ grammatically in speech) to the page, virtual or real. By building foundations of writing based in oracy and in the everyday, writing is demystified: it is not started with a foray into the world of fancy vocabulary and poetic notions. Instead, it is functional and real, where vocabulary matters because of its accuracy and preciseness. Language is beautiful and can be used to evoke any and all of our human emotions, but it does not have to start that way: it can be a layer that is there once the functionality of the writing has been established and made. Again, relate this to the way we talk. If two people describe their experience at the same event, one account may paint a vivid picture which has you doubled up with laughter, while the other is a factually accurate account that is functional but evokes no emotion or carries no humour.

The *Aims for Reading* also make reference to the role of talk by outlining the importance of pupils being able to articulate their views ahead of writing as part of the planning stage:

- Pupils should develop a capacity to explain their understanding of books and other reading, and to prepare their ideas before they write. (DfE, 2013: 3)

This idea of rehearsal is picked up again in the *Aims for Writing* as the basics of transcription and composition are enhanced with the cycle of writing:

- It is essential that teaching develops pupils' competence in these two dimensions [transcription and composition]. In addition, pupils should be taught how to plan, revise and evaluate their writing. (DfE, 2013: 5)

Within these same aims, the connection between transcription and composition is made explicit:

- Writing down ideas fluently depends on effective transcription: that is, on spelling quickly and accurately. Effective composition involves articulating and communicating ideas, and then organising them coherently for the reader. (p.5)

This link between the reader and writer marks the balance we must strike between reading as a writer and writing as a reader. Working in this way, as has been shown through the practical projects you may have seen in school including *Talk for Writing* developed by Pie Corbett and Julia Strong (Talk4Writing, undated) where engagement of the writer with their audience – the reader – is paramount. From the outset, it is the purpose of writing that is stressed as the process of crafting a piece of writing begins. During the course of a unit of work or through a series of lessons, the balance between reading and writing shifts:

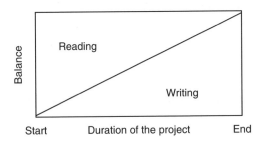

Figure 3.1 Demonstration of the balance between reading and writing

This analysis may feel a little obvious but it needs to be a conscious awareness for teachers and learners if they are to realise the aim of:

- Pupils being taught to control their speaking and writing consciously (p.5).

Purposes for writing

In specific relation to writing, what was once taught through the study of genres in the Primary National Strategy of 2006, is now taught through the study of purposes: **Purposes**

for writing. The shift away from the categorisation of writing through specific genres is an opportunity for purposeful teaching and connected learning. When dealing with a purpose for writing, the writer is not restricted to any particular form of presentation and the element of authorial choice becomes much clearer and more of a reality.

For example, if a class has worked on the writing purpose to inform, the children may have conveyed this through a leaflet, a letter, or a blog update. Here, the writing principle links to the familiar study of reading where texts are analysed and deconstructed. By thinking about instructing and explaining as opposed to instructions and explanations, it becomes easy to see the relevance between the spoken language and writing: explaining is something that forms part of our everyday lives; we explain what happened when things go wrong, we explain how our latest toy or app works, we explain how we have put things together and whether they are creations from building bricks or irrigation systems for the garden. This approach also promotes more discussion and requires more time to be spent on the process of writing, rather than on the product of writing.

Planning for writing

For teachers, planning for writing presents an opportunity to incorporate choice into teaching in a way that is real and manageable. It also means that the learning will need to enable pupils to build and develop their skills for writing, ahead of perfecting the structure of a particular genre, and before subverting or playing with the format. This also encourages teachers to layer the learning, to vary the formats and to ensure pupil choice in the publication of their writing for a wider audience. The next chapter will present a suggested approach to writing that embraces the challenges of the curriculum and its focus on purposes for writing. The second and third sections of this book use this format to offer suggested routes into writing which both reflect the current curriculum aims while being underpinned with a secure pedagogy for writing.

References

Bearne, E and Wolstencroft, H (2007) *Visual Approaches to Teaching Writing*. London: SAGE.

Cremin, T and Myhill, D (2012) *Writing Voices: Creating Communities of Writers*. London: Routledge.

Cook-Gumperz, J (2006) *The Social Construction of Literacy*. Cambridge: Cambridge University Press.

Corbett, P and Strong, J (undated) **www.talk4writing.co.uk** (accessed 15.1.16)

DCSF (2009) *Talk for Writing*. The National Strategies: Primary. London: DSCF.

DfE (2012) *Review of the National Curriculum in England: What we can learn from the English, mathematics and science curricula of high performing jurisdictions.* London: DfE.

DfE (2013) *The National Curriculum.* London: DfE.

DfEE (2000) *Grammar for Writing.* London: DfEE.

DfES (1999) *National Literacy Strategy.* London: DfES.

DfES (2006) *Primary National Strategies – A Framework for Literacy.* London: DfES.

Fisher, R (2006) 'Whose writing is it anyway?', *Cambridge Journal of Education,* 36(2): 193–206.

Myhill, D and Jones, S (2009) How Talk Becomes Text: Investigating the Concept of Oral Rehearsal in Early Years' Classrooms, *British Journal of Educational Studies.* 57(3): 265–284.

Myhill, D, Jones, S and Watson, A (2013) Grammar matters: How teachers' grammatical knowledge impacts on the teaching of writing, *Teaching and Teacher Education,* **36**: 77–91.

OECD The Programme for International Assessment (2012) *Results in Focus: What 15-year-olds Know and What They Can Do with What They Know.* Paris: OECD Publishing.

Smith, F (1982) *Writing and the Writer.* London: Heinemann.

UKLA/PNS (2004) *Raising Boys' Achievement in Writing.* Leicester: UKLA.

4 Teachers as readers and writers

Introduction

This chapter takes a step away from talking about writing and introduces you to a new subject called Design and Technology. And what does Design and Technology have to do with writing? Well, the argument is that the parallels are many; whether it is through reviewing existing products, understanding the market, designing for the sake of it, or just because of a love of design. This what writers do: they immerse themselves in text, know their audience and engage creatively with the writing process – and all because writing does something for them. Whether consciously or subconsciously, both writers and designers follow a similar process: they adopt a schema or utilise a structure made up of distinct component parts. These separate and individual elements all work together to achieve the final result, the assembly of a finished and polished product.

You may be of an age where you remember designing products in primary school, such as a felt purse or a fairground ride. These were well-loved artefacts of the now departed QCA units of work and it may be that some of them can still be found in your parents' loft. What you should also remember from that experience, and as a teacher you must know, is that these projects do not start with the making of a final product. Just as effective writing starts with reading, not with writing, the construction of the product is one of the last parts of the process. Its success is dependent upon the care and attention given to the preceding elements. Jerome Bruner, one of the most influential of the social constructivists, suggested that *knowing is a process not a product* (1996:72). Eve Bearne (2002:6) extended this notion to writing, and posed the question: *Writing: noun or verb?* She challenges practitioners to consider whether writing is either process or product. However, why choose when both parts are important and necessary for the refinement of writing?

Figure 4.1 May (age 5) and lunchtime

Jottings

Review the example below which compares an inventor's approach to the design of a new clock to how a writer might go about crafting a piece of writing. Reflect on a piece of writing you have recently engaged with. This might be something in your current classroom, or even an academic piece of writing of your own. Was this the process you followed? Was one of the components more important than another? Was there one component you would return to in order to spend more time on in order to improve the final piece?

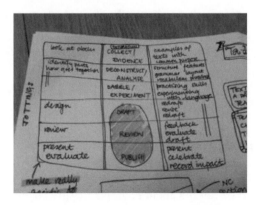

Figure 4.2 A suggested process for writing

What this reflection should leave you with is an understanding of the role of process – and an appreciation of product that you can use and apply in order for children to master the craft of writing, regardless of whether the outcome is a persuasive poster, an entertaining description, or an informative leaflet.

In summary, there is a process to embed in your mind when you plan, when you model, when you scaffold and when you refine the craft of writing. The national curriculum (DfE, 2013) provides a three-part process which is useful: *Plan, Draft and Write,* and also *Evaluate and Edit.* Although this feels a little procedural and a little too linear, it might be useful, in understanding the process to use the additional headings as a framework against which you can quality assure your teaching of writing.

Process components	Questions to ask yourself
• **Saturating**	*Which texts can you immerse readers in to exemplify the purpose for writing?*
• **Deconstructing**	*How will you approach the analysis of the text, to identify and extrapolate the language features of composition and transcription?*
• **Dabbling**	*Where are the opportunities to experiment, choose,practise and play with the language features?*
• **Composing**	*What choices will be made about the language features which best meet the purpose of the writing, in a format that serves the needs of the audience?*

While the argument throughout this book is that reading and writing are interdependent, the following section presents them separately, and heeds the warning of Barrs and Cork (2001).

> *Most people who talk about children 'learning to read and write' seem to assume a relationship between these two activities that can be taken for granted. Indeed, those who practise writing as a profession – novelists, poets and journalists – often say that they read in order to write. This kind of 'everybody knows' assumption lurks in the teaching of writing in school.*
>
> (Barrs and Cork, 2001, p.9)

Teacher as reader

It follows that the more children are exposed to quality texts (including on-screen and through traditional written texts) and by talking about complex picture books, being encouraged to read silently or talking about what they have read, will all impact on writing. Through listening to stories being read aloud and learning from you as an experienced reader, children will come to understand that reading and writing are inextricably linked and begin to develop in children as a *holistic package* (Flynn, 2007:143).

Saturating	*What variety of texts can you can immerse the readers to exemplify the purpose for writing?*
Deconstructing	*How will you approach the analysis of the text, to identify and extrapolate the language features of composition and transcription?*

Research tells us that teachers engage personally with their own reading; however, professionally they draw on too narrow a body of knowledge of reading, often from their own childhood reading (Cremin *et al.*, 2009). Of the 1200 teachers in Cremin *et al.'s* research, only 48% were able to name six good authors, including Roald Dahl, Anne Fine, Michael Morpurgo, Jacqueline Wilson and JK Rowling. You may read that list and recognise the authors as old favourites and it may indeed be a list that reflects your own reading history. However, there are around 10,000 children's books published each year and, therefore, what teachers need to embrace is ensuring children are saturated in quality, contemporary and exciting texts as well as old favourites.

What the Teachers as Readers (Cremin *et al.*, 2009) research also highlighted was the challenge for teachers in knowing where to find quality resources, and having the time to read them.

> *...practitioners may not be sufficiently familiar with a diverse enough range of writers to enable them to foster reader development, make book recommendations to individuals and promote independent reading for pleasure.*
>
> (Cremin *et al.*, 2009, p.4)

Therefore, as a teacher, you need to choose texts that engage children and inspire them to want to read more and read widely – and you too need to take the time to read them. At the end of this chapter, you will be navigated to a list of suggested websites that can help you find these quality texts and, as you browse, challenge yourself to visit one site and choose one unfamiliar title to read with your class.

The easiest way to become familiar with children's literature is to read children's literature. The ideal vehicle for this is by making time each day to read books aloud; books that cover the wide spectrum of genres, including non-fiction, reading on-screen, information texts, stories, poetry, chapter books, classic literature etc. Read aloud every day to children who are in Reception or in Year 6 and *saturate* them with words and language. Barrs and Cork (2001:116) argue that the reading aloud process is a useful way of *foregrounding the tunes and rhythms of the text* which ultimately influence children's writing, as they become embedded in the author's voice and are exposed to new ways of writing styles. Therefore, without actually doing any writing even the most reluctant writer can improve her writing simply by listening to you read. You are the role model, you are the experienced reader in your class and it is from you that children will learn good reading habits. However, as Layne (2015) argues, you need to explain the pedagogy behind the reason you are spending time reading aloud to your class. Yes, it is enjoyable and fun but it is so much more than that.

This is a book about writing and we are spending time talking about reading. The two are interdependent, and as Barrs (2003) suggests *progress in one mode is intimately related to and dependent on progress in another* (p.276). Children need to talk about what they are reading (both at school and at home), what you are reading and to engage in the type of book talk which Aidan Chambers promotes through his *tell me* approach (1993). Children also need to be saturated in the reading experience through a range of texts and this reflects an important stage in the writing process. For example, if the outcome of a unit of work is an explanation text of the life cycle of a caterpillar in order to inform the reader through scientific knowledge, then children need to be exposed to a range of explanation texts. While the national curriculum has created a shift of emphasis for teachers' planning – in that the focus should be on the *'purpose'* of the writing, as in this case the purpose would be 'to inform' or 'to explain' – it is still important for children to be surrounded by the types of texts which might do this job. You might immediately look to an encyclopaedia or to a non-fiction book, but what about the role of film and visual literacy in understanding this very active process of metamorphosis? What about using a book by Vivian French or Nicola Davies where the authors weave the science through a beautifully crafted narrative? Children need to be immersed and saturated in all of these text types. Only then can they make decisions about how they wish to communicate their ideas to the readers and the form they ultimately want it to take.

While research highlights the power of engaging deeply with the text and its influence on writing (Bower, 2011), all too often the criteria for selecting texts for children are different to those employed by an adult when deciding on the next summer read. For example, in school the selection process considers the length of the story, whether it is available online, whether there are sufficient copies to share in guided reading and, sometimes more importantly, the range and accessibility of photocopiable resources. Instead, it should be about the quality of the text, whether it's a read aloud book (just for pleasure with no follow up work other than just listening and enjoying the words), or whether it's a text that will support the children's new learning in some way. These are all decisions that you need to develop your own criteria for.

Having selected the range of texts you are going to share, you need to consider your own subject knowledge of those texts and the specific learning opportunities it affords. This is the *deconstructing* phase of the writing process. At this point, shared reading is a useful strategy, as unlike reading aloud, it will enable you to highlight for the children a specific aspect of the reading or writing process. The children will need to deconstruct and analyse the text with you as their guide or navigator, and therefore your subject knowledge and text, sentence and word level is crucial. You need to talk confidently about the way the author uses language, hooks in the reader, how the text and image can be interpreted and your reflections on the author's intentions. At this stage, you and the children can be likened to explorers, collecting evidence across the range of texts and looking for those key features they will include in their own writing. Essentially, you need to read like a writer and write like a reader.

 ### No excuses

There is no excuse for not being widely read in children's literature.

Over 40 years ago, the Bullock Report *Language for Life* (Bullock,1975) boldly suggested that it was down to teachers to create a community of readers. The same holds true today; it is down to you and your enthusiasm for reading, which will fire up the children in your class to want to read more, and what lights your fire will light theirs.

> *The Bullock Report noted that the teacher who knows books well, who is aware of pupils' interests and reading background and who discusses reading with them will have a significant impact on whether the pupils continue to read for pleasure.*
>
> (Ofsted, 2005:23)

A book is always a route into quality writing: a route in, but it is also a route out, as it exemplifies the destination you and your class of developing writers are heading for. You are the guide and you are the navigator, and the children are the explorers of language, both as readers and writers and they need to learn from you and have the opportunity to learn from each other.

Teacher as writer

The role of teacher as writer has multiple facets and what you should be modelling includes:

- excellence by exemplifying the writing task and illustrating the required and appropriate subject knowledge;

- empathy by illustrating how to overcome common misconceptions;

- emotional intelligence by demonstrating how to return to a piece of writing to further improve and refine it, with no hint of an *'oh that's good enough'* attitude.

Dabbling	Where are the opportunities to experiment, choose, practise and play with language features?
Composing	What choices will be made about the language features which best meet the purpose of writing in a format that serves the needs of the audience?

Dabbling is the start of the drafting process: it allows us to capture and keep treasures as well as refine techniques that we are pleased with and may want to use in our final piece but does not burden us with the entire composition. It is like rehearsing over and over again the 'twiddly bit' in a violin concerto or the 'blahdiblah' of a sonata. You do not need to practise the whole piece, but there are a couple of sections that may need more focus and more refinement, or it may be that at this stage new techniques or patterns need to be employed. *Dabbling* provides the rehearsal time needed to master the 'difficult to articulate' bits of writing, but you know a good piece of writing when you meet it. This is also the time to improvise and veer off the planned route, where children change and explore written language as they develop new ideas (Dombey, 2013). Just like the jazz player whose technique is to stray from the basic melody, so can the confident writer as they dabble and play with words and phrases: What works? What doesn't? What might need changing? It is also at this stage that your role as a writing teacher needs sensitivity. When Jeanne Willis, author of *Tadpole's Promise*, talks to teachers about writing, she talks of the need for a *thoughtful editor, not a harsh critic*. The outcome may well be the same in that the child changes their spelling or refines an idea but it is in the how this is done which will make a difference to how the child views their future relationship with writing.

With our awareness of the vital ingredients and our rehearsal of the techniques ready, so begins the cycle of writing: like the spin of a good washing machine, there will need to be many revolutions through to the process of *composition*. The fewer the cycles, the less developed or finished the writing will be. This has implications for our teaching and learning; the idea that one draft and one polishing session are sufficient may get most children to write, but where is the pursuit of excellence in this model? Books are not published when an author submits the best they can do in a particular time frame and after only one or two attempts. Ask yourself whether you could achieve your very best in just one lesson. Cremin (2006) argues *if teachers engage as writers, taking part in the creative process of composing, they will arguably be in a stronger position to develop the creative voice of the child* (p.4). However, despite this and Bearne's (2002:30) declaration that teachers write in the presence of their classes, there is also evidence to suggest that teachers find this a challenging call to arms. However, when teachers engage in projects which provide a space for them to write as adults, the outcomes suggest they begin to perceive *writing as a means of creating and expressing meaning both in their own lives and the lives of the children* (Grainger, 2005:16). One key role for you as a teacher is to demonstrate 'authenticity' about yourself as a writer, as by sharing your ideas and your anxieties children will more readily share theirs (Cremin and Myhill, 2011:134).

Over to you

This notion of crafting and refinement in the *composition* of writing is best understood when you see it in the context of learning. Watch a short clip called *Austin's Butterfly* (see references at the end of the chapter). The story involves a boy called Austin and how his initial presentation of an accurate and scientific picture of a butterfly adapts and changes according to the feedback he is given.

The clip best illustrates what the researcher Ron Berger (2003) was pursuing – the notion of *beautiful work* or, in other words, we need to expect the very best of children when they write. Berger suggests that Austin forgets to *look like a scientist,* reflected in the first butterfly he draws. He draws from memory rather than observing closely and reflecting this new information in his drawing. But, as he listens and responds to feedback, his drawing improves at an impressive rate. It is not difficult to see how the same metaphor can be applied to a child and her writing. What new information might be shared at the start of a new unit of work? What might she be drawing on to support this new learning? What might we see if we had classrooms of children who 'looked like writers'?

By visualising learning as the top of a swing ball post – the spiralling part (the part where the cord connected to the ball travels up and down and which repeats the same pathway) – a similar thing happens. When we have multiple opportunities to revisit the same area of learning, we do so at a more advanced, developed level. Think about how this relates to learning a new piece of vocabulary. First of all we are unaware that the word exists, then we start to hear it and see it, we experiment with integrating it into our own practice and learn the parameters within which we can use it, and then it begins to makes sense and we learn where it will work and where it's not so useful. Finally, we assimilate it fully into our lexicon and it becomes an embedded part of our vocabulary.

As discussed in Chapter 1, this is what makes writing hard as, unlike other subjects, many things happen simultaneously when we write: we need to focus on our orthography, our clause structure, our sentence demarcation, our paragraph links, our text layout and the overall impact of our writing. At this stage, there should be talk in your classroom, lots of talk: children should be engaging with oral rehearsal or writing aloud (Fisher *et al.,* 2010). What the children are doing is translating their ideas into a written form, and because you know that written and spoken text is different, you understand that to craft a sentence that makes sense both in terms of its content and its grammatical structure, it needs to be heard. By saying aloud what it is you want to write as you say it, you may find that it changes the order of words or phrases and in doing so you refine your thinking. It is only at the point when you are satisfied: that when you write your sentence and then read it back, you may still find yourself having to listen carefully as you read it aloud to check that what you have written makes sense and, most importantly, that it says what you want to communicate to your reader.

The complexity of the process busts one myth: writing is not a magical process. It has axioms to follow that govern and guide the way we compose and transcribe the letters, words, clauses and paragraphs. All too often *good* writing is mystified and accepted as something that you can either do or you cannot, with the suggestion that to be a good writer, magic wands and spells must be at play.

Reflect on the attitude that can accompany the attainment of Level 3 writing at Key Stage 1, Level 6 writing at Key Stage 2 and A* at GCSE level. Children achieving these levels might carry labels like being gifted, talented or natural writers and indeed there are some children who are unaware of how they achieve their outcomes – they just appear to be able to do it. The reality of these 'natural writers' belongs to the comparisons to members who attribute their success to the 10,000 hours rule: a theory proposed by Malcolm Gladwell (2009) in his book *The Outliers*. The existing alumni are people like Wolfgang Amadeus Mozart the musician or Nicola Adams, the boxer, and it is no coincidence that both of these professionals reached the top of their game. It would be more shocking if they had not because of the number of hours practice and tutelage they received, in addition to their personal resilience and determination to succeed. But what of children on the other side of the debate, those Key Stage 2 children who leave primary school not having achieved Level 3? What needs to be provided for them is the same quality that needs to be provided for all: children should be systematically taught how to navigate the journey of further developing as a writer, and this should be exactly the same process for those entering secondary school at level 4 or Level 6. The journey is systematic and structured, navigated by teachers who are inspired role models, who have excellent subject knowledge and who understand that engaging with writing can be powerful but is always personal. There is no black hat, no wand, and no white rabbit.

Text as teacher

Chapter 2 highlighted the importance of children being surrounded by a wide range of texts to support both reading and writing and you were challenged to audit your current provision of quality literature. Text is like a passive or silent teacher, and your job is to train the children to make the text talk to them and engage with them. The only way this will happen is through the establishment of a classroom culture that enables a whole range of feedback, whether it's at a teacher level, or as peer feedback.

TA DAH!

In reviewing the dabblings of 8 year-old Ben (see Figure 1.5, p.11), it was easy to read between the lines and take a guess as to what he may have been reading recently: *The Chronicles of Narnia* (2002), or perhaps *Alice's Adventures in Wonderland* (2015). There was a familiarity about his choice of language, the setting and the sense that we know what might happen next. Ben is demonstrating what Vygotsky reminds us of, that *reading and writing are two halves of the same process* (as cited in Barrs, 2003, 267; Flynn and Stainthorp, 2006). In addition, Cairney (1990) would argue that *each new text written reflects, in some measure, the shadows of texts experienced in the past* (p.484). Therefore, encouraging children to read for pleasure and to enjoy the texts that we as teachers aim to saturate them with and immerse them in, all helps them to become writers.

Reflect back on Ben's writing and what his story told you about what he knows about writing. We could make a list: he knows about fantasy stories, he understands the importance of setting, of suspense, of conjunctions, of typography in his use of CRASH, he knows about punctuation, of beginning/middles/and ends etc. And all the time he's dabbling with this home writing, his text is giving you, as the teacher, a lesson in what writing means to him – in essence the text has become your teacher.

Navigating to quality texts

If you are going to be a teacher of reading and writing who is a role model for the children in your class, you need to know how to navigate your way to quality children's literature. However, teachers are busy with their day jobs, and whilst the most committed teacher will have the will, the skill of navigating to useful resources which can support planning can feel like an art form. The following websites are tried, tested and recommended places that will provide the inspiration for choosing texts you might read and authentic writing events you might plan for.

Book Finder

Book Trust's online *Book Finder* allows you to search by age range and genre. In addition, the site provides a synopsis of the book, together with a biography of the author and/or illustrator.

www.booktrust.org.uk/bookfinder

The Write Book

The Book Trust's most recent writing project *The Write Book* provides ideas for how a class book can get children involved in the power of story, words and pictures. The Write Book teacher toolkit focuses on themes including: engaging reluctant readers and writers, supporting pupils with EAL, the involvement of families and providing ideas for writing projects inside and outside the community.

www.booktrust.org.uk/resources

Core Books Online

CLPE's *Core Books Online* is free to registered users. It contains a comprehensive selection of book titles from ages 3 to 11 and allows you to search by age range, collection, or author. In addition, the site provides ready-created booklists and includes reference to CLPE's unique three collections: *Learning to Read, Literature* and *Information books*.

www.corebooks.org.uk/

Everybody Writes

This Book Trust/National Literacy Trust project ran for four years (2007–2011) and was evaluated by the University of Sheffield as providing a positive impact on pupils, teachers and schools. In particular, the project was deemed to be successful in providing ideas and suggestions for writing activities that support teachers when planning meaningful writing opportunities, often within a real context. Resources, case studies, film clips and interactive tools, including an on-line writing audit are still free and available.

www.booktrust.org.uk/programmes/primary/everybody-writes/

National Literacy Trust Network membership

The National Literacy Trust Network supports individuals and schools to develop outstanding literacy provision by providing literacy leaders with tools, resources and inspiration.

www.literacytrust.org.uk/network

Power of Reading

CLPE's Power of Reading website is used in conjunction with the training they provide to support both the transformation of a school's reading culture and the reinvigoration of a school's literacy curriculum.

http://por.clpe.org.uk/

The remainder of this book draws together these ideas through the exemplification of lesson plans which are both thematic and subject-based and which will provide authentic and creative opportunities for the developing writers in your class.

References

Austin's Butterfly (film clip on youtube) https://www.youtube.com/watch?v=hqh1MRWZjms

Barrs, M and Cork, V (2001) *The Reader in the Writer*. London: CLPE.

Barrs, M (2003) The Reader in the Writer, in Grainger, T (ed.) (2003) *The RoutledgeFalmer Reader in Language and Literacy*. London: Routledge.

Bearne, E (2002) *Making Progress in Writing*. London: RoutledgeFalmer.

Berger, R (2003) *An Ethic of Excellence: Building a Culture of Craftsmanship with Students*. London: Heinemann.

Bruner, JS (1966) *Toward a Theory of Instruction*. Cambridge, MA: Belknap Press.

Bower, V (2011) *Enhancing Children's Writing, Creative Ways to Teach Literacy*. London: SAGE.

Bullock, A (1975) *The Bullock Report: A Language for Life*. London: Her Majesty's Stationery Office.

Cairney, T (1990) Intertextuality: Infections Echoes from the Past. *The Reading Teacher*, 43(7): 478–484.

Carroll, L (2015) *Alice's Adventures in Wonderland*. London: Macmillan.

Chambers, A (1993) *Tell Me: Children, reading and talk*. Portland, ME: Stenhouse Publishers.

Cremin, T (2006) Creativity, Uncertainty and Discomfort: Teachers as Writers. *Cambridge Journal of Education*, 36(3): 415–433.

Cremin, T and Myhill, D (2011) *Writing Voices: Creating Communities of Writers*. London: Routledge.

Cremin, T, Mottram, M, Collins, F, Powell, S and Safford, K (2009) Teachers as Readers: Building Communities of Readers, *Literacy*, 43(1): 11–19.

Dombey, H (2013) *Teaching Writing: What the Evidence Says*. Leicester: UKLA.

Fisher, R, Jones, S, Larkin, S and Myhill, D (2010) *Using Talk to Support Writing*. London: SAGE.

Flynn, N (2007) 'What do effective teachers of literacy do? Subject knowledge and pedagogical choices for literacy', *Literacy*, 41 (3) pp.137–47.

Flynn, N and Stainthorp, R (2006) *The Learning and Teaching of Reading and Writing*. Bognor Regis: John Wiley & Sons Ltd.

Gladwell, M (2009) *The Outliers: A Story of Success*. London: Penguin.

Grainger, T (2005) Teachers as Writers: Learning Together. *English in Education*, 39(1): 75–87.

Layne, S (2015) *In Defense of Read-Aloud: Sustaining Practice*. Portland, ME: Stenhouse Publishers.

Lewis, CS (2002) *The Chronicles of Narnia*. London: HarperCollins.

Ofsted (2005) *English 2000-5 A Review of the Inspection Evidence*, Report 2351. London: Ofsted.

Wills, J (2005) *Tadpole's Promise*. London: Andersen Press.

5 Becoming a historical enquirer

Navigation

Purpose of the writing: To inform

Context: Link with history and the lives of significant individuals in the past

Destination and audience

The aim is to create an information tent card or luggage tag as might be found in a museum to label a Victorian artefact. Consider making a visit to a local museum or creating your own museum, create a role-play area based on a Victorian lost property office. The children will need to make decisions about what does/doesn't belong to a visiting time-traveller who needs help in re-packing his suitcase. The luggage tags/tent cards should include justifications for the children's decisions made, for example, *'This should be in your case because...'* The tags or cards will form part of a classroom display and the audience will be other children and classroom visitors.

Backpacks of practice

- Knowledge of local history, and achievements within my family/own life.

- Prior knowledge of previous history topics and being a historical enquirer

- Being good at asking questions, formulating questions and finding ways of answering them.

- Note taking and caption writing skills acquired in subjects such as geography, science and through early mark-making and written annotations.

- Possible knowledge of time travel through films such as *Mr Peabody and Sherman* or through television programmes including the *Horrible Histories* series, or experience of books in the *Charlie and Bandit* or *Harry and the Bucketful of Dinosaurs* series.

Teachers' toolkit:

- Time-specific terminology
- First/second/third person
- Chronological framework
- Similarities and differences
- Use of adjectives
- Simple conjunctions: *because, but, if, and*
- Formulating questions
- Structuring an answer to posed questions, both verbally and in written form and being able to discuss the differences in used grammar.

The blurb

In this writing plan, Year 1 children will be contextualising their knowledge of information writing within a historical topic. The aim was to gather information about what it is like to live in the Victorian time of 1837–1901, during this era of great national achievements. In the history national curriculum (for England and Wales), children are taught about the lives of significant individuals, and there are many famous Victorians to choose from: Isambard Kingdom Brunel, Charles Dickens, Florence Nightingale or Mary Seacole. Alternatively, in learning about life beyond living memory, the focus could be on the introduction of mandatory and then free schooling which all took place in Victorian times – and this will be the focus of this writing plan.

Older children travelling back to Victorian times could arrive on a specific date when something was invented and proved to be a significant turning point in British history: for example, the penny-farthing bicycle, the postage stamp, the telephone, or even the earliest type of text message – the telegram. Did you know that the Victorians enjoyed a sweet tooth, and this was the era when ice cream, jelly babies and even the Easter egg came to prominence? As well as practical inventions and tasty sweet things, this was also the era of social responsibility, with no fewer than 640 charities being in existence in 1861: the Barnardo's charity was founded through the work of Dr Thomas Barnardo, while the Ragged Schools attempted to teach working class children for free, and both The Salvation Army and the Children's Society were established. It was also the time of great children's literature, many of the following titles are likely to be much-loved books in your school library: *The Water Babies*, *Alice's Adventures in Wonderland*, *The Wonderful Wizard of Oz*, as well as the work of Charles Dickens.

Choosing the starting point for your time travel should not pose too much of a problem. Having arrived back at your chosen date, the children need to gather as much information as possible in order to help a nineteenth-century time-traveller who has found himself trapped in your twenty-first century classroom. The precursor for the children's writing is the use of drama, and in particular role play through strategies such as hot seating, the mantle of the expert and teacher-in-role.

Why this would inspire

Figure 5.1 The Victorian time-traveller

For young children to write effectively they need to have a knowledge of both the topic and the purpose for the writing. For the Victorians history topic, it is easier to have an understanding of what life was like many years ago. We are surrounded by artefacts, buildings and institutions that still exist and children can touch and experience history through their fingertips. In other topics, such as *The Great Fire of London* or *The Story of Christopher Columbus*, there is a greater challenge, both geographically and conceptually. (Therefore, seeking out strategies that provide a *way in* to children's curiosity – and help them to understand the notion of a different time but in the same place – are essential.)

Family and friends are very important to teachers, as they can often take on the role of numerous unknown characters who suddenly arrive in classrooms ready to share a historical fact or a scientific finding. Of course, as with any drama activity children are asked to suspend disbelief – something that any kind of imaginative play encourages. If you decide not to call on family and friends, then simply the addition of a top hat, or putting on a pair of glasses indicates to the children that your role is different: you are no longer their twenty-first century teacher but a reporter, or maybe an RSPCA animal carer. This is something that children do themselves in the role-play corner, or when engaged in their own playtime games. In this writing plan, the Victorian time-traveller arrives in the classroom unable to return to his own time, unless the children can help.

Figure 5.2 Thomas Barnardo in class

In this image, we can imagine the pioneer and campaigner Thomas Barnardo marvelling at the reading abilities of a Year 1 child. Maybe as he listens, he compares the achievements of this boy with the chances and opportunities that children have within his own time and right across Victoria's reign. In order for the children to learn more about school life in the last century and to get a sense of historical time and place, using drama strategies enables children to enter into an imagined world. Within this writing activity there are two suggested strategies: mantle of the expert and hot seating.

1. Mantle of the expert

Dorothy Heathcote is the great exponent of this strategy, which she referred to as a dramatic inquiry-based approach to teaching and learning. The idea is that the whole class (including the teacher) take on the role of imagined experts, which could mean the class are scientists discovering DNA or astronauts working on a mission to Mars. The key difference is that the children assume roles, rather than taking on a part in a play. Their talk becomes natural and they take on the various responsibilities required as part of the activity or problem they are trying to solve. For very young children, talking about their own experiences of school with the Victorian time-traveller will allow them to become the expert: they can share their knowledge of learning in the classroom and of playground games. By taking on this role with the classroom visitor they naturally adapt the way they use language. They adopt school-type terminology, provide explanations and clarify any misunderstandings. To further expand on this experience, the hot-seating activity develops the conversation so that the children begin to learn from the visitor.

2. Hot seating

At its simplest, hot seating is a strategy where someone in class takes on the persona of another, for example the Wizard in *The Wizard Oz*, or the White Rabbit in *Alice in Wonderland*. However, when taking on the role of a historical figure, rather than a fictional one, it is important to avoid choosing the key figure, for example, not Queen Victoria or Thomas Barnardo. This avoids a child asking the question, 'How did you feel, Thomas, when you made the decision not to go to China?', and 'Thomas' not knowing how to answer it, because your visitor hadn't rehearsed that bit of the life story. If, instead, the character in role is Thomas' assistant, or even Victoria's servant, then answering the questions is easy, as it leads to responses such as 'I would imagine he/she felt…', rather than the children expecting the definite answer. The use of hot seating also requires the children to formulate the kinds of questions that require extended answers, which in turn leads them to justifying their responses.

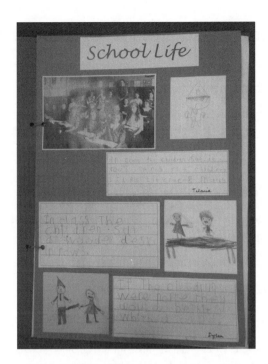

Figure 5.3 School life writing

Figure 5.4 Book about the Victorians

Prior knowledge and previous learning

 Backpacks of practice

Before starting this writing topic, find out what children already know – their skills and prior knowledge.

Children may have had:

- practice of creating labels, captions in formal learning;

- opportunities to write in informal settings through literate role-play activities, including writing notes, labels, invitations etc.;

- experience of rehearsing sentences and how to turn an idea into a sentence;

- opportunities to make comparisons and using comparative and superlative adjectives (-er and -est);

  Previous experiences:

  o Children may have been to a gallery/museum or exhibition where there are caption cards to explain what the visitor is looking at. In school, there may even be display cabinets in the foyer which has caption cards for uniform or school trophies.

The plan		
Day/context		Year 1
Link with Victorian topic and the lives of significant individuals		
Purpose	Audience	Format
To inform	Formal, unknown	Non-chronological report, captions

National Curriculum links
SPOKEN LANGUAGE
Ask relevant questions to extend their understanding and knowledge
Articulate and justify answers, arguments and opinions
Participate in discussions, presentations, performances, role play, improvisations and debates
READING
Drawing on what they already know or on background information and vocabulary provided by the teacher
Participate in discussion about what is read to them, taking turns and listening to what others say
Explain clearly their understanding of what is read to them

WRITING – composition

Draft and write by:

Write sentences by:

Saying out loud what they are going to write about

Composing a sentence orally before writing it

Sequencing sentences to form short narratives

Re-reading what they have written to check that it makes sense

Discuss what they have written with the teacher or other pupils

Read aloud their writing clearly enough to be heard by their peers and the teacher

WRITING – vocabulary, grammar and punctuation

Join words and joining clauses using and

Begin to punctuate sentences using a capital letter and a full stop, question mark or exclamation mark

 Hook ~ Visit by a Victorian time traveller

Learning Objective and Success Criteria

We are learning to:

Write an information caption to label an artefact

Success Criteria:

- I can describe an object
- I can name an object
- I can decide if an object belongs to the visitor or me
- I can give reasons for what I think
- I can write my idea as a sentence

Starter

Have a range of everyday objects on the carpet with a view to discussing the objects' characteristics. Children to pick up the objects and start to explore them.

Have two prompt questions: What is it made of? What shape is it?

What other questions can we ask?

Capture the vocabulary: longest, biggest, smallest, newest, oldest etc.

Write the vocabulary on individual pieces of card then ask the children where it goes as they begin to classify the objects and vocabulary according to size, shape, material, age.

Discrete learning: using the suffixes –er and –est

Key questions:

Which is the biggest? Which is the smallest?

Which is the oldest?

Which is the newest?

Which is bigger than another?

Introduce a range of found artefacts from the present day and Victorian England; the artefacts are grouped with two Victorian artefacts and one modern item.

Children to describe what they see, and see if they can compare the objects. Example sentence: *'The jug is round and made of china. The stick is wooden and long and thin'*.

Note: the children may be able to describe an artefact but not know its name. Decide when and how to introduce the names of the artefacts.

Children need to devise an oral sentence to describe their object including *'and'*. Pair up with another, then compare the differences and similarities between the two artefacts *'Both of our objects are round but yours is made of wood and yours is thin and mine is fat.'*

Input

Using two suitcases (one modern and one from the Victorian era) the children need to create tent cards with a sentence describing and naming their artefact. Explain that the Victorian suitcase belongs to a Victorian gentleman who knows Thomas Barnardo. The children decide whether their artefact and tent card need to go in the modern or Victorian suitcase. Children need to be using the vocabulary introduced in the starter input.

Differentiation

Lower attainers	*Middle attainers*	*Higher attainers*
Oral rehearsal is used to practise their sentence	Sentences...	Paragraph...
Initial sounds for words	Children write a sentence to describe their artefact.	Children write a sentence introducing their artefact.
Discuss comparisons between two artefacts.		Describe it and compare it to another.

Plenary

Introduce Chester, who is a Victorian time traveller who has got lost in time. He needs to return to the time of Thomas Barnardo so that he can help him establish the ragged schools. It is very important that no one knows Chester is a time traveller, so he must take nothing back that belongs in the wrong century. The children need to help Chester make the right decisions about which artefacts go in his suitcase and which ones remain behind. Encourage the children to justify their choices using *'because, but and if'*.

'If Chester takes the plastic spoon it would be useful because he could use it again and again, but they would know he was a time traveller because plastic was not invented then'.

Taking your bearings

In order to be confident in introducing these writing ideas it is important to stop and take your bearings and reflect on your own subject knowledge. For example,

- You need to know about the history of both the present day artefacts and the Victorian artefacts. For example, if a child wants to include a plastic spoon in the Victorian suitcase, it is important for you to know that plastic was not invented until 1907. Equally, understanding how a dolly-stick was used is as important as knowing what it is called.

- The children need to discuss their ideas with each other and the adults in order to move their oral expression into a complete idea, before it becomes a written sentence. Children in Year 1 will readily share fragments of ideas, or useful words, but they need support in using their 'collection of ideas' to create an oral draft sentence before it becomes a sentence on a page. Adopt a strategy of 'say it, say it again, say it as you write it and say it having written it'.

- Children should be encouraged to generate vocabulary through the use of prompt questions that provide scaffolding for their sentences.

- Capture the words and ideas in order to create a word bank as a reference. This will either be used for independent transcription or to support better quality description. The teacher will need to clarify some descriptions, for example *'it's a bit roundy'* could be improved by providing a more precise adjective for example, *curved* or *rounded*.

- It might be that children do know what the artefacts are called because of prior learning; however it is still possible to describe an artefact without knowing what it is called. Therefore, description should come first in both the oral and written sentence work with the name of the artefact coming at the end. Encourage the children to come up with their own name for the artefact, as the Victorians often used quite creative terminology.

- The stages of learning will be children working collaboratively and orally to discuss, compare and describe their artefact. The children will then work with the teacher who scaffolds the collation of their ideas through the actual artefact and the use of sticky notes to collect and create a word bank to describe the artefact.

- In order to show evidence of both the learning journey and pupil progress, children should be able to choose which artefact they describe in their books. They will need a selection of photographs to choose from, to stick in their book before capturing the vocabulary to describe their artefacts.

- Children will work independently or with an adult to create a tent card that has the artefact's description and name. The writing plan outlines the differentiation of this task.

- The text structure:

  o introduce the artefact;

  o describe the artefact;

  o compare the artefact;

  o name the artefact;

  o designate to a present-day or Victorian suitcase.

→

Examples of children's writing

Figure 5.5 School life display

Personalising the plan

Teachers' toolkit

Some children will need further support in turning their ideas into written sentences. Using a blank line scaffold highlights to children the rhythm of a sentence and how it translates into words, which in turn can become a discussion about known words and initial sounds. It is also an opportunity to allow the child to select words they think might be tricky. For example, they may know some of the historical vocabulary because of prior learning or through exposure to classroom word banks. The use of the blank line scaffold allows you to establish what the child knows in terms of their spelling knowledge, syntactic understanding and use of punctuation. It should be combined with the 'say it, say it again, say it as you write it and say it having written it' strategy.

The writing activity could be used at the start of a unit or in the middle in order to assess the children's historical knowledge and understanding. For example, can they identify the 'red herring' items

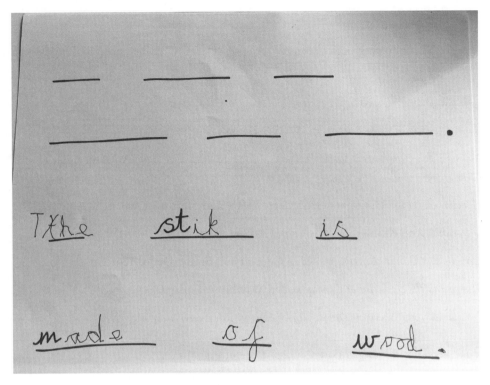

Figure 5.6 Blank line scaffold

that are not matched to this period of history? This allows children the opportunity to extend their spoken language by justifying their answers and responding to the contributions of others. In turn it takes the focus of the learning away from individual written responses into a purposeful discussion based on dialogic talk. Talking tins could be used to capture the ideas and sentences of children who might not be able to write them independently.

This activity is ideally suited to support children who may have English as an Additional Language, or for those with communication difficulties, because the vocabulary can be translated into Makaton or Widget symbols. In addition, children could attribute characteristics of different arte-facts using pre-prepared labels with comparative adjectives/superlative adjectives on them. Key to this activity is the use of talk to support the decision-making process and scaffold their sentence construction.

To extend higher-attaining children, they should be encouraged to create paragraphs that first describe their article and then compare the similarities and differences with the artefacts in their group of three, or an artefact from the alternative suitcase. They could also be encouraged to justify why their artefact belongs in the present day or Victorian era.

Routes in

The following books/resources are useful starting points when looking for routes into the topic.

- *Role play activities, such as hot seating and mantle of the expert.*

- *Stone Age Boy*, Satoshi Kitamura. Walker Books (2008)

- *You wouldn't want to be a Victorian (series)*, John Malam and Dave Antram. Book House (2014).

- *Horrible Histories: Victorians (series)*, Terry Deary and Martin Brown. Scholastic (2013).

- *Victorians*, Ann Kramer. DK Children (2011).

- *Charlie and Bandit Adventures*, Kelly Gerrard and Emma Dodd. Templar (2011).

- *Harry and the Bucketful of Dinosaurs*, Ian Whybrow. Puffin (2003).

- *Mr Peabody and Sherman* Dreamworks Animation (film)

Abridged versions of many children's classics including:

- *Alice's Adventures in Wonderland*, Lewis Carroll. Macmillan (2015).

- *The Water Babies*, Charles Kingsley. Collins (2012).

- *The Wonderful Wizard of Oz*, L Frank Baum. OUP (2015).

- *The Secret Garden*, Frances Hodgson Burnett. Faber and Faber (2015) (first published in 1911, but based in the Victorian era).

An animated biography of Charles Dickens

https://www.youtube.com/watch?v=unKuZ2wlNdw

Visit the History Shed at the Literacy Shed: includes links to Pathé News, Queen Victorian's Journals and BBC resources

https://www.literacyshed.com/the-history-shed.html

6 Creating a geographical soundscape

Navigation

Purpose of the writing: To communicate, to inform

Context: Soundscape narrative linked to oral storytelling

Destination and audience

To create a narrative soundscape that captures the journey from school to a familiar place in the local environment. To communicate information about the journey's route by describing what can be seen and heard to share with other class members. The creation of a story narrative with the aim of painting a picture with sound through words. The audience may be the local community, parents invited to a classroom assembly, or a class or year group.

Backpacks of practice

- Experience of telling stories

- Small World© play

→

- Going on and describing journeys both near and far

- Experience of familiar known stories that have a journey element.

Teachers' toolkit:

- Technical vocabulary, including subject-specific vocabulary relating to both human and physical geography

- Oral explanations, and labels and captions that can be created from visual representations and maps.

The blurb

Within this teaching sequence, the children will be experiencing different ways of doing something familiar and habitual. What might be a simple and regular journey on a normal day, whether on foot or in the car, will become an expedition or an adventure and will evolve into a journey that stays with you. What is seen, heard and smelled becomes important – and it is this reliance on the senses that will lead to a description of the familiar.

The aim is for the children to combine their experience of storytelling with the specific vocabulary of geography. While the link with writing may not seem obvious, any activity that involves children going outside the classroom and experiencing an event ensures they have something to write about, and subsequently they write better. The element of story is something that children are familiar with: they tell stories of their play, of significant events of their lives, and even the most straightforward request from their teacher often leads to lengthy descriptive responses full of suspense, dilemma and tension. The focus of this activity is the translation of an experienced event into a visual representation through simple mapping techniques that will ultimately lead to a musical interpretation. It is important to see the link to writing, both through the notion of a narrative genre needing beginnings, middles and ends, but also in the way in which children turn ideas into visual representation. It just so happens that the visual in this instance is an annotated map, but it could just as easily be through written words and sentences.

Using familiar stories such as *We're going on a bear hunt*, *Handa's Surprise* or *Rosie's Walk* provides a very simple structure of one of the seven story types, i.e. the quest. Upper Key Stage 2 children could be asked to create a more complex narrative of their journey to school, while children in Year 3 or 4 could use the map as the background to stories set in familiar settings. Other less well-known stories like *Naughty Bus* and *Slam* disrupt the simple idea of a journey, by sending buses hurtling through plates of baked beans, or have main characters who are so plugged into their headphones that they fail to notice anything happening around them. *The Day of Ahmed's Secret* also uses the quest storyline – as Ahmed is sent out on deliveries around the streets of Cairo, but with a plot twist which sees him bringing back something special from each of the shopkeepers.

Older children could use on-line resources like the soundscapes provided by the Barbican's *Can I have a word?* project. The idea of linking key vocabulary, sounds and images is another way of encouraging children to play with language and to find creative ways of communicating ideas. Roger McGough's *The Sound Collector* is a list poem, and his own reading, available via the BBC website, provides children with an example of performance poetry that they can aspire to.

Why this would inspire

Learning beyond the classroom is a known inspiration for writing. The journeys from school do not need to be far, as what this teaching sequence aims to do is to heighten the experience of the familiar by watching and listening. There is an opportunity to combine both geography and English expectations of simple fieldwork and simple observational skills by contextualising the learning with a real experience of the surrounding environment.

Figure 6.1 Sound sticks

Before you head off on the fieldtrip, it is a good idea to collect together a bank of suitable sticks. This avoids every child bringing in sticks from home – you might end up with boughs from trees, rather than the hand-held sticks you had planned for. You will need to take sticky tape, wool and cotton thread with you so the children have ways of 'fixing' the items to their journey sticks (see *Primary Geography Handbook Extension Project – Maps and Stories* in '**Routes in**' at the end of this chapter). The physical markers you collect could be things found along the way, for example, a feather, a stone, a leaf or flower, or you might take a box of trinkets that the children choose from. Some teachers use sequins to represent quantity or colour: three red sequins represent three lampposts while a blue sequin represents a big puddle.

The experience of collecting these physical markers along the way ensures the children remember what a key place looked like and what they heard and smelled there. With a completed stick in hand, the children can retell their journey as a story and orally rehearse sentences to create a reimagined narrative. Encourage them to add flavour and character to their stories: the action and suspense of what happened at the pelican crossing; the balance of short and long sentences; or maybe they can use questions to draw in the reader and add sound effects as precursors for

Figure 6.2 Searching for sticks

their soundscapes. While this activity is not concerned with a writing outcome, the process of saying aloud their sentences is useful practice for when they do turn to writing stories. This information can then translate into an annotated map, complete with captions referencing specific geographic vocabulary: *west, a large tree with conkers*. Immediately, there are sounds associated with the reverberation of conkers falling to the ground or one being hit against another, or maybe the chosen sound represents the rustling of horse chestnut leaves. Provide an orchestra of instruments, both conventional and the junk variety: tin cans, lentil-filled shakers, aluminium foil, sandpaper, cardboard tubes, and let the children add sounds to their journeys.

As with all music, it needs to be performed: it requires an audience to listen, and this is much the same with any piece of writing. Accessing free software is a way of blending in technology through the creation of individual or group sound recordings. The recordings can then be played as the children retrace their steps along their maps, recalling their journeys and practising their newly-learned vocabulary.

Prior knowledge and previous learning

Backpacks of practice

Before starting this writing topic, find out what children already know – their skills and prior knowledge.

Children may have:

- knowledge of the local environment through journeys to and from school;
- familiarity of stories, poems and rhymes based in familiar settings;
- experience of creating informal map-making and annotations;
- opportunities for storytelling in the water play or sand play area;
- experience of creating of captions and label writing in role-play area;
- read non-fiction books and storybooks with journeys as a theme;

  Previous experiences:

- knowledge of maps through exploring on holidays or on car journeys;
- visits to local area;
- exploring the playground;
- stories being read aloud at home.

The plan		
Day/context		**Year 2**
Link with geography topic and local fieldwork		
Purpose	**Audience**	**Format**
To communicate, to create	Informal, known	An annotated journey map and soundscape

National Curriculum links

SPOKEN LANGUAGE

Give well-structured descriptions, explanations and narratives for different purposes, including for expressing feelings

Maintain attention and participate actively in collaborative conversations, staying on topic and initiating and responding to comments

Use spoken language to develop understanding through speculating, hypothesising, imagining and exploring ideas

Gain, maintain and monitor the interest of the listener(s)

READING

Discuss the sequence of events in books and how items of information are related

Become increasingly familiar with and retelling a wider range of stories, fairy stories and traditional tales

Make inferences on the basis of what is being said and done

WRITING – composition

Draft and write by:

Write narratives about personal experiences and those of others (real and fictional)

Plan or say out loud what they are going to write about

Write down ideas and/or key words, including new vocabulary

Encapsulate what they want to say, sentence by sentence

 Hook ~ A fieldtrip journey to a place in the local environment

Learning Objective and Success Criteria

We are learning to:

Write an information text

Success Criteria:

- I can orally recount my journey to a favourite place
- I can visually represent the sequence of my journey

- I can tell the story of my journey using journey stick prompts
- I can add appropriate percussion to my journey
- I can perform my journey soundscape

Starter

Following on from the fieldtrip to a favourite and local place, the children work in pairs to share their memories of the journey. Ask the children to record their favourite memories on paper – at this point there is no expectation that the children have sequenced the journey. What they want to capture are the BIG and IMPORTANT moments.

Each pair to join another pair and ask the children to recount their journeys using their journey sticks and stress that they need to engage the listener.

Teacher to move around the classroom listening in and collecting good examples of where the listener has been drawn in to the recount. Come back together and discuss what you noticed, ask for volunteers to share their favourite parts.

Using the photographs (pack for each group of 4), ask the children to sequence the journey and to cross reference with their own maps. Questions: What happened first? What parts might they have missed out? Find ways of annotating their own map with the correct sequence and give time for the children to add in any missing features. Emphasise the need to label the different journey parts with appropriate words/phrases 'the big green oak tree', 'the barbed wire that tried to catch my coat'.

Input

Using the children's draft annotated and sequenced map, share the percussion instruments that they can use to represent the different parts of the journey. If they want to create their own sound using everyday objects then discuss that as an option.

The children need to use their maps and the instruments to work towards orchestrating a soundscape where the music best represents that stage in the journey.

Children to work in pairs.

Differentiation

Lower attainers	Middle attainers	Higher attainers
Work with an adult as a scribe to sequence the journey – emphasise the use of spoken language. Focus on the appropriate descriptive vocabulary and noun phrases.	Create annotated captions for each key place on the journey. Emphasise the use of adjectives and adverbs to describe what and how something happened. Include use of expanded noun phrases.	Consider using sentences to label the journey using adjectives and adverbial phrases. Include sentences with different forms: statements, questions, exclamations.

Plenary

In groups, children to perform their soundscapes to each other – use the opportunity to compare the annotated map with the final soundscape. How might they be improved? Which percussion instruments worked best? Are there alternatives that might create a better mood? Children to share their journey sticks and their decisions about both annotations and what they collected on the journey.

Taking your bearings

In order to be confident in introducing these writing ideas it is important to stop and take your bearings and reflect on your own subject knowledge. For example,

- You need to be confident in taking children's learning beyond the classroom walls. (Ensure you follow the school's Health and Safety policy and complete the required risk assessments.).

- Walk your planned route a number of times and approach it in different ways: experience the journey through the eyes of a six year old; be as observant on the way there as on the way back; film the journey at low level and notice what you see. Take photographs so that you can prepare packs for the children to use in class as a useful sequencing activity.

- Plan in your own stopping points, but be confident that the children will find their own places of interest.

- Brief the adults who support the trip by highlighting the points of interest you want them to alert the children to. Provide them with prompt question cards: *What can you see if you look closely? Who else has found…? If we use our magnifying glasses what do you notice?* Create word banks of descriptors that can be shared with parents.

- The focus of the classroom work is on spoken language both formal and informal. Children will share their ideas in pairs before working with another pair. It is important to set up Ground Rules for these activities to help the children support each other and encourage ideas. Rules such as: *Take it in turns; Look at the person who is speaking; Speak in a clear voice* are useful and could be laminated onto card as a visual prompt. Encourage the children to use words and phrases such as '*I think…*', '*I agree…*', '*Because…*'.

- Children can be encouraged to see the link between spoken language and writing as they practise the narrative of their journey sticks. The emphasis is on oral rehearsal and the engagement of the listener through gestures and facial expressions. Higher-attaining children can begin to make links between punctuation we use when speaking and written punctuation.

- Create colour-coded cards (blue for subordination; red for co-ordination). As a child retells their journey present them with a differentiated card so they include a specific conjunction (such as *when, if that, because* and *or, and, but*).

- The drama of the journey can be intensified through sentence variety including short ones, image-filled ones and lengthy ones. Use sentences with different forms including: statements, exclamations and questions.

- Let the children practise the retelling of the journey in both the present and past tense and let them hear which is the language of storytelling.

- The sequence of lessons takes the children from a simple recounting, to an embellished story through to the translation of written ideas into sounds. As the children progress through the stages, they should see the links with the drafting and dabbling phases of the writing process.

This can be highlighted through their descriptions of objects or journey stopping points – encourage them to see the move from a noun, to a noun phrase, to an expanded noun phrase. Ask them to consider why the final version creates a clear image for the listener or reader. Look for opportunities in shared and guided reading texts to illustrate where authors have used the same technique.

- Linking the words and music provides an opportunity for performance and will support children in understanding the requirements of a formal situation for an audience. The children will be both performers and listeners and they should be encouraged to both participate and respond to what they hear and enjoy.

Personalising the plan

Teachers' toolkit

This type of activity is one that can be differentiated to support children who may find the transcription element of writing difficult. The emphasis on spoken language and the oral retelling of stories that are based on familiar things and the everyday encourages the children to take ownership of the final written output. Writing in this activity is part of the process and, therefore, should take pressure off children who may find handwriting physically difficult, or for those who

Figure 6.3 Sound stick searching

→

struggle to get their ideas down on paper. The multisensory approach also draws together the interdependency of reading, writing and spoken language that is a key message throughout this book. Linking words and music through common percussive elements also enables children to orchestrate words and sounds in a creative way. The activity can also support higher-attaining pupils as they can extend their vocabulary through their first draft noun descriptions before being encouraged to seek out opportunities to develop their imaginations through expanded noun phrases.

Routes in

 The following books/resources are useful starting points when looking for routes into the topic.

A fieldwork trip to an area within the local environment, the school grounds, the local park, local shops; the walk needs to be significant.

Noticing things that are big and small.

Use of building bricks to create a vehicle that goes on a journey across the sand or water play area.

The Day of Ahmed's Secret, Florence Parry Heide and Judith Heide Gilland. Puffin (1997).

Slam, Adam Stower. Templar Publishing (2005).

The Naughty Bus, Jan Oke. Littleknowall Publishing (2005).

Hurricane, David Wiesner. Houghton Mifflin (2014).

Mirror, Jeannie Baker. Walker (2010).

Red Riding Hood, Various.

Handa's Surprise, Eileen Browne. Scholastic (2006).

Rosie's Walk, Pat Hutchinson. Little Simon (2015).

We're Going on a Bearhunt, Michael Rosen and Helen Oxenbury. Walker Books (1993).

Primary Geography Handbook Extension Project – maps and stories (4-7)

www.geography.org.uk/projects/primaryhandbook/mapsandstories/4-7/#top

Teachers TV: Journey sticks   Jane Whittle

https://www.tes.com/teaching-resource/teachers-tv-journey-sticks-6048401

The Sound Collector   Performed by Roger McGough

www.bbc.co.uk/education/clips/zc6qxnb

Can I have a word?   Visual soundscape of water

www.barbican.org.uk/canihaveaword/

Listening to a soundscape

https://www.youtube.com/watch?v=w5s7FxE64bA

Adding and subtracting sounds to tune in and listen carefully

**https://www.exploratorium.edu/listen/activities/soundscapes/deploy/activity_
soundscapes.php**

The Bumper Book of Storytelling, Pie Corbett. Clown Publishing (2006).

Talking to the Earth, Gordon McLellan. Capall Bann Publishing (1995).

7 Story stones for telling stories

Navigation

Purpose of the writing: To entertain, to narrate and to describe

Context: Using a set of seven stones as a structure for creating a narrative

Destination and audience

In this chapter children will be writing a story based on the main features of an adventurous, spooky or suspense story using story stones as a scaffold. They will craft their completed narrative for performance and publication for an unknown audience which may include parents or other class members.

Backpacks of practice

- Experience of telling stories, of listening to stories and of explaining reading preferences.

- Role-play storytelling by using props and puppets to retell stories.

- Map making, creating own doodles and drawings, and using words to capture the essence of stories.

Teachers' toolkit

- Some children will need further support in turning their ideas into written sentences. Narrative-associated vocabulary including knowledge of story structure.

- A meta-language for responding to children's ideas and improving a piece of draft writing's key features.

- A familiarity with a range of children's stories and quality literature.

The blurb

The use of story stones is a creative response to the ongoing challenge for teachers to make story writing exciting and incremental. Of all the writing genres, story writing or narrative is the most consistent, and every year children are asked to think of new stories and exciting plots to engage and excite an unknown reader. The story stones are simply a set of symbols that represent key plot lines, characters or settings – and while this session uses only seven stones, it is possible to create smaller stone families. For example, each of the seven stones could have a set of adjectives used to describe the characteristics of places or people.

If your school follows a model of storytelling by Pie Corbett (2006), you will already be familiar with the notion of imitating, innovating and inventing known stories. Having learned a story like Little Red Riding Hood off by heart and created a story map to scaffold the retelling, the next step would be to innovate on the practised story pattern by changing different elements. Instead of the story being set in the forest, it might be in a city or out in space. Instead of a wolf, the baddie might be an alien creature. The final step, and this is more often for older children, would be to invent a story using only the known features of the storyline, which in this case would be a quest. This unpacking of a story's structure enables children to take a basic recipe and to add their own ingredients according to their tastes or preferences. There is autonomy about this process – and one that allows the children to 'own' their ideas while using a structure that supports the retelling of stories. It doesn't matter if the story changes in the retelling: stories were originally performed and they were only ever written down for an unknown audience. There is a power in writing a story where your name is on the front and you are the recognised author. Milly's published story of *The Islands of Snow* was displayed in the class reading corner, and to attract her audience she reminds them that it's '*Book 1, 3 chapters long*'. Milly knows that readers need to know what's coming in a book: she captures this most charmingly, and any reader is going to be keen to pick up this book.

The use of scaffolds as prompts is common in classrooms and maybe your school uses a story mountain structure which outlines a five-part process when planning a story: Opening, Build-up, Complication, Resolution and Ending (**www.talk4writing.co.uk**). This is a

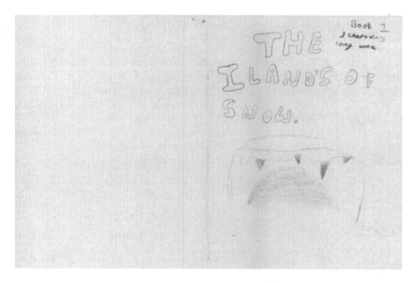

Figure 7.1 Milly's The Islands of Snow chapter book

useful structure but, like any scaffold that supports a building, at some point the scaffold needs to be removed. What we hope remains is a confident and developing young writer who has mastered a new technique. Other strategies, such as story maps, story charts or flowcharts, are other ways of doing essentially the same thing: they allow the writer to plan out what is going to happen in the story, who the main character is, what problems need to be solved, and the challenges to be overcome. This way of pre-planning suits those who like to be organised, but it can be a little frustrating to those who just want to get on and write. George R.R. Martin suggests there are two types of writers, the *gardeners* and the *architects*. The architects plan and consider the whole picture, whereas the gardeners look at what they have to hand, the tools, the ideas and the necessary bit of magic – and they are happy to adapt and create as they go. His stories are not suitable for your primary classes, but you may have heard of his most famous book series *A Song of Ice and Fire,* probably better known as the TV series *Game of Thrones*. Finding ways to support both the story architect and the story gardener remains a challenge: it is easier to teach the architects and to support their planning process. The gardeners might need additional time and space to create their stories and it is usually a messier process.

The link between reading and writing is crucial. This point is stressed throughout this book. Emily's writing, which we first met in Chapter 1, demonstrates this through a piece of unaided story writing that she completed at home. As readers, we have already considered what she knows about writing, but let's return again to one of the phrases she uses. As a six year old, she has already begun to use language in creative ways: the grown-ups weren't 'safe and sound' in bed but '*soft and sound*'. It may have been a mistake, but we get the sense that Emily's spelling is good enough to have tried a word like 'safe', but what she has done is to

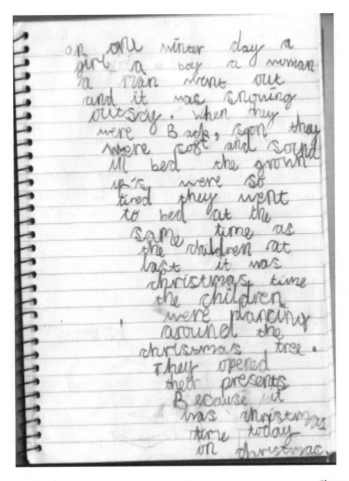

Figure 7.2 Emily's writing

create a lovely image for her reader. We don't know, but we also imagine that Emily likes reading and that she's collecting words and phrases and ideas as she goes. As with teaching, there are no new ideas in writing, but there are an infinite number of ways of adapting and crafting those ideas to create something new and unique. Narrative writing and its myriad of different genres will capture all of your children at some point – it's a question of finding what interests them and how you can bring it into the classroom. Emily writes about what she knows: her story is home-based and has characters that sound suspiciously like parents. This reveals a key implication for you when you are planning story writing. For example, if when planning a unit of work on the Ancient Egyptians, you might see that there is a link between history and narrative writing of myths and legends, or possibly adventure stories. But to do both things well – to know about the Egyptians and to know how to write an adventure story – children first need to be filled up with facts. It is too much to ask an eight-year-old to absorb the history of Egypt while mastering the ingredients of an adventure story all at the same time. Slowing down and familiarising them with the factual detail first, maybe through the creation of information booklets or a curated museum, allows the knowledge to embed before moving onto the specific genre that will result in a fact-filled adventure story full of intriguing twists and turns.

Christopher Booker (2005) argues that there are only seven basic plots in story writing for whatever the age of reader or writer: overcoming the monster, rags to riches, the quest, voyage and return, comedy, tragedy and rebirth. Some are easier to relate to children's experience of story. For example, *Cinderella* is an obvious rags-to-riches tale but remember alternative versions can add an interesting twist, for example *Mufaro's Beautiful Daughters* provides the familiar tale but is set in an African country. *Goldilocks and the Three Bears* is possibly an example of voyage and return, while *Hansel and Gretel* is a good fit for overcoming the monster. The quest is possibly one of the most familiar plots in primary story writing: some of the journeys are geographical like *Handa's Surprise* or *Naughty Bus,* while others might be more of a metaphorical or an emotional quest, as in the *Harry Potter* series, or Gary Paulson's *Hatchet*. Rebirth sounds a little grand, but many traditional fairy tales involve the changing fates of a character's situation, for example, the rather literal rebirth of *Snow White*, or the influence of kindness on the trapped prince in *Beauty and the Beast*, or reflected in Mary's transformation in *The Secret Garden*. If you're scratching your head trying to think of other stories which fit the plotline, see Babcock LDP Primary Literacy Team's set of blueprints which suggest other contemporary texts that teach the different plot types (see Routes in at the end of this chapter). Included in the *Seven Basic Plots blog* list: *Tadpole's Promise* as a Key Stage 1 tragedy; *The Invention of Hugo Cabret* as a modern-day fantasy rags-to-riches tale, and picture books are included, with *Shortcut* by David Macaulay suggested as an example of a comedy.

Why this would inspire

Just one of the challenges for teachers when planning for story writing, or a narrative unit, is to understand the various layers and component parts that are required before even thinking of asking children to turn the page and write a story. Writing is not just speech written down, and this is especially true with story writing where grammar changes, conventions are less formal and the combination of description, dialogue, recount, dilemmas, problems and resolutions – as well as possibly a moral message – all have to be juggled.

Presuming that all of the above have been mastered, the next step is to find different ways of teaching about story structure, especially if your school has an agreed format. If, after five years in school, the story mountain is used in the same way as when it was first introduced in Year 1 there are not going to be too many enthused Year 6 writers ready to show you their potential.

Teacher: *What do you need if you're going to write?*

Child: *A pen and an idea.*

What the story stones activity attempts to do is to capture a plot line, but in such a way that it addresses the needs of both the architects and the gardeners. The story stones also provide a tangible connection to the story, whether the children are deconstructing a known text or creating their own. The senses are involved, making it a visual, auditory and tactile experience. The more the children immerse themselves in the creation of a story by using the stones to swap around, to adapt the build-up, or to dramatically change the resolution, the more likely they are to remember it. There is an ownership in retelling, even if it's the retelling of a story that's been heard a hundred times before – 'Yes, but in this version of Chicken Licken, the sky really does fall in and the story starts right after this has happened'. Think of the endless possibilities.

The story stones are also accessible and lead to self-differentiation. On a practical level, the children are creating their own story vocabulary. They can transfer the created images or symbols onto the stones using permanent markers, paint or even collaging their pictures. When dry, the stones can be coated with PVA glue to give them a lasting quality, and as they get ready to decant the seven stones into a wallet, the children are already considering the potential of their story. Simply rolling out the stones on a story map leads to the challenge of creating as many different narratives as possible, or the story stones could be set against a story mountain with the stones providing inspiration at the various different stages, or any potential changes. Perhaps Goldilocks lives with the bears and has swapped places with baby bear? Perhaps the three bears have come to Goldilocks' house? The children can work in pairs on separate mountains and try to merge the stories together. This immediately disrupts the traditional story mountain format, leading to an alternative and more potentially more creative ending.

The story stones can also be used in reverse, by providing the children with a collection of pre-prepared stones depicting a well-known story. Depending on the chosen images, it is possible to make it harder – or easier – for the children to predict the story and to identify its genre. All of this playing with order and structure, possibility and potential, reveals to the children that story ideas are not hard to come up with, it's the *what happens next* that's the difficult part. Any teacher will have had the experience of a child writing a cracking opening full of suspense, drama and intrigue, only for the story to fall flat in the middle (with the exception of a list of names of their friends, or possibly a car chase) before a final sentence appears to tidily resolve the story, or the inclusion of the '… and it was all a dream' sequence: a phrase that turns even the most creative of teachers' blood to ice. To avoid this scenario, seek out creative ways of deconstructing texts, of saturating children with quality literature and allow them the time and space to dabble throughout the composition process. By the time the children are ready for writing, you want them writing with ideas popping and stories ready to explode.

Prior knowledge and previous learning

Backpacks of practice

Before starting this writing topic, find out what children already know in terms of their skills and prior knowledge.

Children may have knowledge of:

- stories, poems and rhymes based in familiar settings;

- enjoyment of a range of wordless picture books;

- listening to adults read aloud;

- joining in when adults read aloud;

- writing at home, creating stories and short chapter books to share;

    They may also have previous experience of:

    o   film tie-ins of known and popular stories;

    o   visiting libraries for story reading;

    o   receiving books from various book gifting schemes, e.g. Book Start, Booktouch, Bookshine, Young Readers Programme;

    o   involvement with projects such as Book Time, The Ant Club, Summer Reading Challenge, Premier League Reading Stars;

    o   playing in the role-play area, telling stories with puppets or props.

The plan Day/context Link with storytelling and story writing		Year 3
Purpose	**Audience**	**Format**
To entertain, to narrate, to describe	Formal performance	Narrative genre: adventure, spooky or suspense
National Curriculum links SPOKEN LANGUAGE Articulate and justify answers, arguments and opinions Use spoken language to develop understanding through speculating, hypothesising, imagining and exploring ideas Speak audibly and fluently with an increasing command of Standard English		

READING

Identify themes and conventions in a wide range of books

Discuss words and phrases that capture the reader's interest and imagination

Draw inferences such as inferring characters' feelings, thoughts and motives from their actions, and justifying inferences with evidence

Predict what might happen from details stated and implied

WRITING – composition

Plan

Discuss writing similar to that which they are planning to write in order to understand and learn from its structure, vocabulary and grammar

Discuss and record ideas

Draft and write

Compose and rehearse sentences orally (including dialogue), progressively building a varied and rich vocabulary and an increasing range of sentence structures

Narratives, creating settings, character and plot

Evaluate and edit

Read aloud their own writing, to a group or the whole class, using appropriate intonation and controlling the tone and volume so that the meaning is clear.

 Hook ~ Using and designing a set of story stones

Learning Objective and Success Criteria

We are learning to:

Write an information text

Success Criteria:

- I can identify the features of a known narrative genre
- I can understand how symbols and signs represent sections and features of a story
- I can discuss reasons for my choices
- I can respond to questions about my choices
- I can create a set of symbols to represent features of my chosen narrative genre

Starter

Share a set of story stones or an image of one. Explain how each of the images on the stones can represent different things so they can be used to inspire stories, each set containing hundreds of possibilities. They could signify plot points, characters, settings or events. Show a stone with an eye on it and explain how many different ways this could serve as inspiration for a story – it could be a magical eye that can see through walls, it could signify that a character in a story saw something happen, it could mean our hero is being watched...

⟶

Input

Part one

Split children in to small groups and give each a story stone. On big paper, they generate as many ideas as possible for what their stone could signify in a short time. They choose one meaning and write it on a piece of A4 paper with a large sketch of their stone.

Each group chooses a representative who shows their chosen stone to the class and shares one of their ideas. Collect these on the board.

Part two

Ask the children to draw 10 stone shapes on a piece of paper (or provide a sheet with these drawn on). The children now use this sheet as a design sheet to plan out some different ideas for their own set of seven story stones. Model the sketching out of ideas – they should be simple symbols, not whole stories in their own right. Leave a screen on the smart board or a sheet on tables showing some ideas prompts: weather, places, buildings, people, creatures, objects and symbols.

Differentiation

Lower attainers	Middle attainers	Higher attainers
Work with an adult to identify the main features of a known story and create a spider diagram to collect ideas.	Create a set of story stones using a known fairytale. Work through an illustrated storybook to support them with the step-by-step of narrative.	Prepare a set of question prompt cards for use with a partner. Encourage discussion in the plenary based on justification for inclusion of only seven of their ideas.

Plenary

Children to share their sketches with a partner and together they decide which seven designs would work best as story stones. Encourage discussion, questioning and justification of ideas. The criteria for choosing should favour simplicity and images that could carry multiple meanings.

Taking your bearings

In order to be confident in introducing these writing ideas it is important to stop and take your bearings and reflect on your own subject knowledge. For example,

- You need to understand the language of story including: plot, character, setting and events. An awareness of the importance of the role of specific narrative style including suspense, adventure and spooky stories. Refer to *Grammar for Writing* (2000) for useful prompts for 'writerly knowledge'.

- Be aware of children's barriers into story writing, whether it's a difficulty with capturing ideas, transcribing the ideas or performing their finished stories.

- Have knowledge of the types of strategies that can support children in capturing the story voices, whether through assistive technology or providing additional adult support.

- Planning effectively across the unit of work allows the necessary time and space to *Plan, Draft and Edit* and *Evaluate and Edit* writing.

- Understand that the suggested three-part process for writing is complex; break the *Draft and Edit* stage into smaller process components: saturating, deconstructing, dabbling and composing.

- Appreciate the seven basic plots and their associated vocabularies, and consider where plots are most appropriate across the age range.

- Have confidence to write in in front of the children with your ideas not fully formed.

- Have a repertoire of websites, books and resources that re-present similar ideas in new and exciting ways.

- Shared writing is an essential strategy in storywriting. Being able to demonstrate what comes next and how to refine and edit writing is crucial to children seeing that writing isn't just something that appears by magic.

- Make writing messy and show children first drafts of work by prolific authors like Roald Dahl, Beatrix Potter and Malorie Blackman.

- Know how to respond to writing, as you are the piece's first audience. Read the writing with the child and show interest by talking about specific ideas and asking questions. Involve the child, what are they most proud of, what would they change, what's the best part?

- Don't be afraid to talk about the areas that need improving but be selective about the mistakes that need correcting and provide a purpose for any re-drafting, for example, tailoring to suit a specific audience or further transcriptional editing prior to publication.

Personalising the plan

Teachers' toolkit

Many of the strategies shared within other chapters in this book can be applied here to support pupils or to extend those who are able writers. This section focuses on strategies you may wish to employ with children for whom writing presents specific barriers, for example, those who have a specific learning difference and find transcription challenging, or those who have a sensory impairment and need access to assistive technology. While all genres of writing may pose challenges for children in these specific groups, there is something very personal about writing a story. Creating a newspaper report, or writing a recount of a trip or planning a science experiment feel different and they lend themselves to working collaboratively or involve an adult's translation of ideas.

→

Story writing provides children with the chance to have their voice heard: it is often a very personal response.

For children who have ideas for writing, but find writing those ideas down difficult, the planning stage is very important. The story stones provide a useful structure for helping children to hold onto their ideas rather than losing them as they begin to write. It is important to allow time for children to practise reordering the stones and talk about why they have made their choices. This will support them in embedding the story in their long-term memory with less likelihood that they'll forget what comes next. It is frustrating for a child to know that they have good ideas for writing but that they find it difficult to capture them. Removing the pressure will open up the opportunities to keep thinking ahead.

Making use of recording software on iPads or tablets gives immediacy to a child's voice in ways that writing by hand takes longer to capture. There is a range of freely available applications, such as the Open University's *Our Story*, which combines images, sound and text where the child takes on the role of author or composer. The *Our Story* app could be the next step for children as they begin to structure their story – each story stone could become one shot within the filmstrip, which is then populated with text and voice recordings as they reach the final stage of developing the story detail. Children with a visual impairment or a hearing loss can also make use of these types of assistive technologies to further develop their story ideas.

As the story stones are merely symbols, it is easy to create the symbols with raised line drawings for children with a visual impairment. The triangular symbol that represents a mountain, or the stick tree that represents a forest are only 2-D representations and are not pretending to be compared to a real mountain or tree. The fact that the stones are tactile and can be categorised according to shape can provide further scaffolding. For example, the set of seven stones can be one size, while the connected families of characteristics are smaller and, therefore, more physically recognisable.

A child with a hearing impairment is unlikely to have grasped the notion of rhythm and pattern solely through aural skills; they will have watched the faces of the reader, felt the tapping out of the story or joined in as the words were acted out in which they took a full and active part. While the child may have no difficulty in writing down their stories, you do want them to engage in discussions around their ideas so that they adapt their thinking and further develop their vocabulary repertoire. Pairing children up with an appropriate talk role model can provide them with the experience of having their ideas heard by an empathic listener. This needs to take place in a classroom environment that embraces talk and dialogic experiences so that it is not anything different for the child, but part of everyday classroom practice. Using the stones as story stepping-stones can create gaps in the story structure, and where there is a gap (it could be a blank stone) the child has to fill it with their own prediction as to what might happen. This encourages the child to look not only ahead but back at what has happened from the other teller's point of view, which helps them to keep the sense of the story's journey. Accessing local authority sensory support teams is also another way of engaging the experts, and will further support the children but will strengthen your pedagogy at opening up the world of stories to all children in your class.

Routes in

The following books/resources are useful starting points when looking for routes into the topic.

Storyboxes and a Storysack© (see Chapter 12) can offer a creative way-in for children to role-play storytelling of familiar stories, using prompts and puppets to support in the retelling. Literary role-play areas can provide a space for children to play with the story language: they can change the outcome and practise performing and developing confidence in the specifics of story language.

Red Riding Hood, Various

Goldilock and the Three Bears, Various

Hansel and Gretel, Various

Chicken Licken, Jonathan Allen. Corgi Childrens (1997).

Mufaro's Beautiful Daughters, John Steptoe. Puffin (1997).

Shortcut, David Macaulay. Houghton Mifflin (2001).

Tadpole's Promise, Jeanne Willis. Andersen Press (2005).

The Invention of Hugo Cabret, Brian Selznick. Scholastic (2007).

The Secret Garden, Frances Hodgson Burnett. Vintage Children's Classics (2012).

The Harry Potter series, JK Rowling, Bloomsbury Children's Books (1997–2007).

Hatchet, Gary Paulson. Macmillan's Children's Books (2005).

Naughty Bus, Jan Oke. Little Knowall Publishing (2005).

Handa's Surprise, Eileen Browne. Scholastic (2006).

References

Booker, C (2005) *The Seven Basic Plots: Why We Tell Stories.* London: Continuum.

Corbett, P (2006) *The Bumper Book of Storytelling into Writing* (Key Stages 1 and 2). Wiltshire: Clown Publishing.

DfEE (2000) *Grammar for Writing.* London: DfEE

Available as a downloadable PDF

http://webarchive.nationalarchives.gov.uk/20100612050234/nationalstrategies.standards.dcsf.gov.uk/node/153924

The Story Starter Shed

https://www.literacyshed.com/the-story-starter-shed.html

Babcock LDP Primary Literacy Team – a set of blueprints, or texts that teach

http://literacyresourcesandideas.edublogs.org/category/seven-basic-plots/

Resources, case studies and ideas

www.talk4writing.co.uk/

(free to join the Network)

Our Story – the Open University

www.open.ac.uk/creet/main/projects/our-story

8 Using quality children's literature

Navigation

Purpose of the writing: To persuade, to entertain

Context: Writing letters to Dumbledore

Destination and audience

Each child will write a letter, written on parchment paper and delivered by Owl Post to Albus Dumbledore. The purpose of the letter is to apply to join one of the four Hogwarts houses and to demonstrate that they have the required characteristics to be a valued member for the house. Dumbledore will make his decisions and write back to let applicants know if they have been successful, as it will determine Quidditch teams for later in the term.

Backpacks of practice

- Knowledge of Harry Potter series both in print and through film.

- Links with other magical reading either read independently or shared with another adult: *The Lion, the Witch and the Wardrobe*; *The Velveteen Rabbit*; *Northern Lights: His Dark Materials*, or *The Magic Finger*.

→

- Creative play and imagination through own magical experiences; spell writing or making garden-based potions of rose petals and slugs.

Teachers' toolkit:

- Use and shape anecdotes, being able to provide opening statement and supporting evidence.

- Use inference and deduction when looking for clues in reading.

- Transference of reading skills into writing.

- Modelling of writing through shared writing.

- Use paragraphs, expanded noun phrases, modal verbs and adverbs to indicate range of possibility and persuasion.

The blurb

Children's quality literature not only offers children the chance to surround themselves with a rich tapestry of words while opening a door to their imaginations, it also provides the perfect foil for writing. Projects such as *The Write Book* (Book Trust), *The Power of Reading* (CLPE) and *Everybody Writes* (Book Trust) demonstrate the potential of texts as a stimulus for quality writing. For those children who find the idea of writing a story and facing a blank page a daunting prospect, using a known text offers a welcome structure – while being fuelled with ideas enjoyed through the eyes of the author's text construction. Equally, the child who loves reading and whiles away hours embracing fantasy worlds and constructing their own creative responses will relish the opportunity to further delve into characters' lives and their imagined worlds.

While this chapter draws on a fictional response, through the use of the hugely popular Harry Potter book *Harry Potter and the Philosopher's Stone*, the principles can equally be applied to both non-fiction texts and non-fiction responses. For example, using picture books like *Bringing the Rain to Kapiti Plain* or *Handa's Hen* – books that follow a familiar repetitive narrative structure and on first reading are simple folk tales – contain within them a wealth of information about the shared experiences of children's lives in other countries. Therefore, a non-fiction response in the form of a postcard, letter, or simply a list of journey elements of their own lives offers a non-fiction response to a story. Equally, an information text, such as *A First Book of Nature* by Nicola Davies, would allow a lower Key Stage 2 child to respond both creatively to the subject and allow them freedom over the form. For example, *A First Book of Nature* contains recipes, poetry and facts, as well as illustrating how captured souvenirs from nature walks can be scrapbooked. Increasingly, these kinds of texts challenge the conventional fiction/non-fiction divide and are sometimes referred to as 'hybrid' texts, as they cross genre boundaries where content and structure can be hard to define. Building in the use of texts such as *Yucky Worms* (Vivian French) and *The Emperor's Egg* (Martin Jenkins), can involve the children in choosing how they respond, highlighting the notion of choice as an important element in any planning for writing.

The national curriculum (DfE, 2013) refers to the importance of reading, as it *feeds pupils' imagination and opens up a treasure house of wonder and joy for curious young minds* (p.4) and, therefore, this chapter will demonstrate how quality children's literature can support exciting and engaging writing.

Figure 8.1 Owl post

Why this would inspire

Imagine a lively Year 5 classroom: the children have just returned to class after a busy break-time when their teacher, Miss Williams, walks in with a large parcel wrapped in brown paper and tied up with string. The children are intrigued as she proceeds to sit down at her desk before silently reading the address, '*Attention – The Owls*' and as an aside she comments out loud, '*Who, I wonder, could this be from?*' This now has all the children's attention and they return to their desks awaiting her next move. She unties the string, removes the paper and places the contents (a larger, padded envelope) on her lap and slowly, and quite painfully for the children, she refolds the brown paper before placing it on her desk. The children at the back strain forward with heads bobbing both left and right trying to see over the shoulders of their friends, while those at the front quickly realise that the feathers that appear to be escaping from the parcel can be caught. They jump from their seats and begin to grasp at the feathers that float towards them but then elude them as another attempt fails to grab them. Instead the feathers float above their heads before settling on shoulders and desks while a few feathers make it to the ground before being rescued by excited young writers.

This was the scene that took place in a Year 5 classroom as they received individually-addressed letters from Dumbledore, in envelopes sealed with red sealing wax and engraved with a handheld 'H' seal. The letters were written on parchment by PGCE students who were replying to the children's letters to Dumbledore requesting they be considered as potential candidates for one of the four Hogwarts houses.

Dear Professor Dumbledore,

As you are the most powerfull wizard ever to live, I am writing to assure you that I will be the perfect pupil for Slytherin. I have thought this out thoroughly and it is my final decision.

Hopefully, this writing shall prove to you I belong in Slytherin. Last year, when I was ten, (behind my parents' back) I locked my brother in his room and would not let him out until he let me use his wand. I got severely punished for my sneaky abilities.

I will therefore continue to be as sly as a snake like I have already shown, if you put me in Slytherin, also in year seven I will lead young minds in the RIGHT direction.

Yours sincerley, Peeter

Figure 8.2 Peter's writing

The letters had been bundled up in the larger, padded envelope and stained with tea, slightly burned at the edges with feathers attached and labelled 'By Owl Post'. The fact that the class of children were also called Owls was one of those serendipities that always seem to happen in the very best of classrooms.

Dear Professor Dumbledore,

I am writing to inform you that I have become the magical age of eleven and to tell you that I wish to be in Hufflepuff. Yes, I have been thinking very deeply and it has occurred to me that this is the house best suited to my talents. I would therefore like to share my skills with you.

Hopefully this does not sound arrogant, but I will say that I am quite sharp-minded and a hard worker. At my ordinary school, I have conquered level 6 and achieved level 7 in mathematics, literacy and reading due to my hard work and concentration. I am not afraid of a challenge, like Hercules and I am democratic; I will never leave a man behind. My kind and fair traits improve on my social life. Even though I do like to complete my tasks, I can be extremely patient.

In conclusion, I believe that I am worthy of admission and hope to see you soon.

Yours truly,
George

Figure 8.3 George's writing

Prior knowledge and previous learning

Backpacks of practice

Before starting this writing topic, find out what children already know – their skills and prior knowledge.

Children may have:

- written or received letters or postcards both imaginary – to the Tooth Fairy, Father Christmas – or to family members or friends;

- written a School Council manifesto 'Why you should vote for me';

- experience of justifying whether they were or were not in trouble; persuading parents they should stay up late or receive a particular gift;

- recounted to parents or adults in charge how something had happened, how something had been broken, how a sibling's fingers might have been caught in a door;

    Previous experiences:

    o they may have watched the Harry Potter films, read the books or listened to the audio books;

    o visited Warner Brothers Studios, seen YouTube videos;

    o written magical spells;

    o taken part in magical lessons.

The plan		
Day/context		Year 5
Links to 'Magical Mayhem' topic for this half term.		
Purpose	Audience	Format
To persuade, to entertain	Formal, unknown	Letter, anecdote
National Curriculum links		
SPOKEN LANGUAGE		
Give well-structured descriptions, explanations and narratives for different purposes, including for expressing feelings		
READING		
Draw inferences such as inferring characters' feelings, thoughts and motives from their actions, and justifying inferences with evidence		
Provide reasoned justification for their views		

WRITING – composition

Draft and write by:

Select appropriate grammar and vocabulary, understanding how such choices can change and enhance meaning

Use a wide range of devices to build cohesion within and across paragraphs

Proof-read for spelling and punctuation errors

Perform their own compositions, using appropriate intonation, volume and movement so that meaning is clear

WRITING – vocabulary, grammar and punctuation

Recognise vocabulary and structures that are appropriate for formal speech and writing, including subjunctive forms

Use expanded noun phrases to convey complicated information concisely

Use modal verbs or adverbs to indicate degrees of possibility

Use commas to clarify meaning or avoid ambiguity in writing

 Hook ~ Owl Post, letters to Dumbledore!

Learning Objective and Success Criteria

We are learning to:

Write an anecdote.

Success Criteria:

- I can match an incident to a characteristic
- I can structure sentences to describe actions in the simple past and past continuous
- I can structure a sequence of sentences to recount an incident
- I can use a variety of sentences openers to indicate time
- I can use a variety of sentence openers to indicate causal relationships
- I can describe what makes an effective anecdote and include this in my own example.

Starter

Recap the key events of 'The Sorting Hat' chapter of *Harry Potter and the Philosopher's Stone*, read last week.

Q: What are the main events of the chapter?

Q: Using all the evidence available, can you tell me what you know about the Sorting Hat and the role it plays in dividing the new students into the Hogwarts houses?

Children to be divided into four groups, each representing one of the four Hogwarts houses, using a pack of cards (clubs for Gryffindor, diamonds for Hufflepuff etc.).

Look at the working wall to remind you of the characteristics of the characters associated with each of the four houses.

→

Word sort:

Each table has 3 words which you would associate with the following characters:

Harry, Malfoy, Crab, Hermione, Neville, Luna Lovegood

Words: cunning, clever, determined, ambitious, eccentric, sly, clumsy, serious, studious

Use sticky notes to add more of your own ideas.

Input

Model creating a situation that best illustrates one of the character + a characteristic.

For example, Malfoy + devious = Once in a potion-making class, he swapped Ron's wand for the teacher's wand, ending up causing a large explosion which Ron was blamed for.

Now model the same characteristic applied to yourself:

I don't have a wand and I haven't been to a potion-making class but I have been devious. Give an anecdote of a time that you were devious. In order to demonstrate this, use a limited number of words to convey a series of events. Model this using the 3-part sequence.

Introduce: Once when I was 9, I put a snake in my sister's bed.

Develop: Upon discovering it, she screamed like a baby.

Consequence: When my dad found out, he stopped my pocket money for 3 years.

Think, pair, share – children practise choosing one of the characteristics from their chosen house and an incident that best exemplifies this. Have a go at writing the anecdote.

Children return to their tables to review their letters from yesterday. They need to consider where they might insert the anecdote that will evidence for Dumbledore that they are the ideal candidate for their chosen house. See workshop differentiation below.

Differentiation

Lower attainers	Middle attainers	Higher attainers
Range of anecdote starter/concluders on pieces of card (colour-coded): Once when I was… You'll never believe what happened… In the end… Finally…	Identify the expanded noun phrase, which conveys the key information about the incident(s). Vocabulary mat and thesaurus to improve the quality of their chosen characteristics.	Have a discussion about the examined anecdotes and categorise effective/non-effective examples. Determine what is required to paint a picture with words concisely and precisely. Children to write their own.

Plenary

In learning threes, children to rehearse, perform and to receive feedback before giving their final performance. Peers to evaluate against lesson success criteria.

Taking your bearings

In order to be confident in introducing these writing ideas it is important to stop and take your bearings and reflect on your own subject knowledge. For example,

- You need to know the features of persuasive writing and the importance of conveying information in a concise and entertaining manner.

- To understand the features of persuasive texts using letter writing as a tool through:

  o use of simple present tense and the past tense to give examples exemplifying their application;

  o use of causal connectives *if, therefore, as a result, this shows*;

  o use of conditional structure using different verb tenses *'If I were to be considered Malfoyesque enough, I would live up to this by...'*;

  o include movement from the generic to the specific illustrated with examples;

  o use adverbials for time, place, manner.

- Use devices to build cohesion within a paragraph and link ideas across paragraphs.

- Understand how writing is different from spoken language demonstrated through the introduction and conclusion of the letter.

- Analyse similar text types to inform the planning and structure of children's own work. Using real world examples of letter applications for jobs, recounts of anecdotes and how the reader has been engaged, reviewing job descriptions and matching skills and experience and examples of letters for different purposes: information, entertainment, communication.

- Review and agree the attributes required for entry into one of the four houses based on evidence from the text (either book or film) and the children's own ideas and interpretations. Encourage the children to be specific and concise in their reasoning and justification.

- Children should be encouraged to make individual decisions about their house choice based on things that have happened in their lives. Encourage everyday talk to justify their reasoning, share anecdotes and shape their ideas through partner talk and clarification.

- Y5 writing moves children onto the structured cycle of planning, drafting, evaluating and editing and this needs to be scaffolded by a confident teacher who can demonstrate all stages of the writing process.

- Use shared writing as a strategy for modelling the planning and drafting process. Pre-film another teacher talking to camera about their house choice including anecdotes shared in everyday language. Challenge the children to capture the salient points and include comments on body language and non-verbal cues. Discuss with the children how the key information was conveyed and how this translates into the written form.

- Model for the children how you arrange the oral ideas into writing that precisely captures your reasons. Children need to be made aware that this process includes capturing, drafting

→

and redrafting ideas, both within the sentence and across sentences and paragraphs. Discuss what information comes first, whether it is sufficiently persuasive and its impact on the reader. For example, in spoken language it is easy to use face and hand gestures to convey emotions, but in writing the author needs to make deliberate decisions about which device to use, for example through the use of an exclamation mark, a piece of dialogue or an exaggerated description.

- Devise a shared rubric for the letter that meets the requirements of the task e.g. paragraphs that convey different reasons for the house allocation and how those paragraphs can be built, structured and linked.

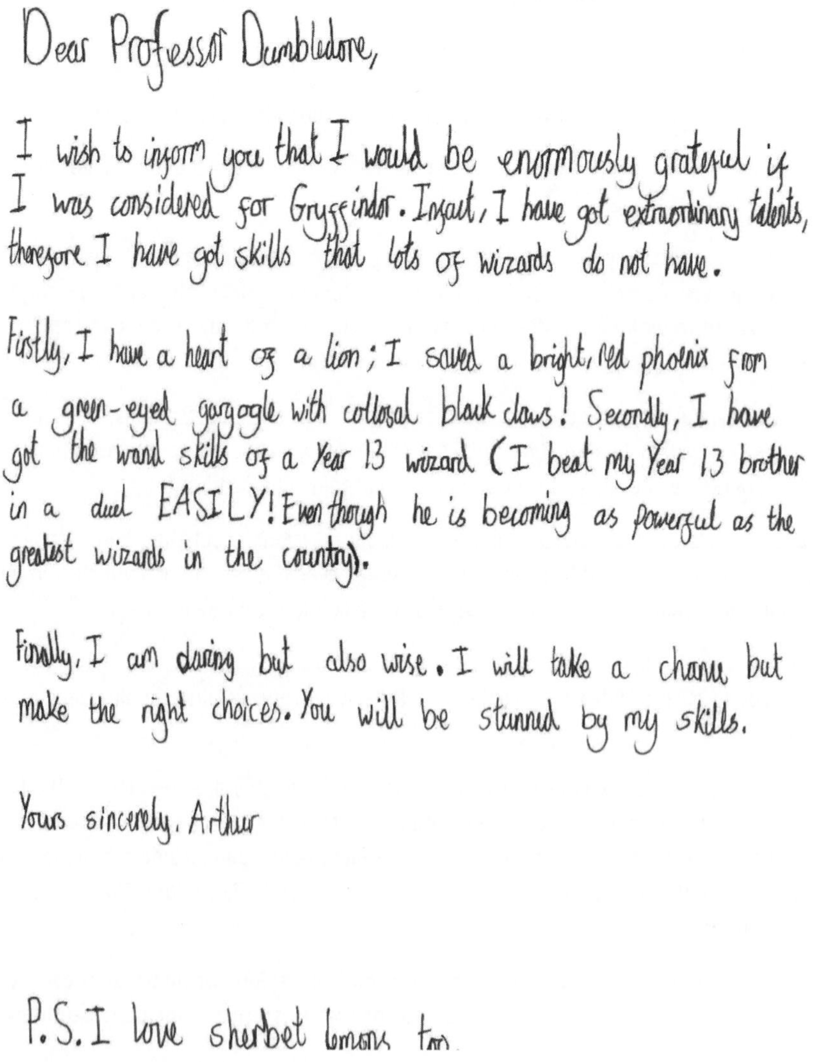

Dear Professor Dumbledore,

I wish to inform you that I would be enormously grateful if I was considered for Gryffindor. Infact, I have got extraordinary talents, therefore I have got skills that lots of wizards do not have.

Firstly, I have a heart of a lion; I saved a bright, red phoenix from a green-eyed gargogle with collosal black claws! Secondly, I have got the wand skills of a Year 13 wizard (I beat my Year 13 brother in a duel EASILY! Even though he is becoming as powerful as the greatest wizards in the country).

Finally, I am daring but also wise. I will take a chance but make the right choices. You will be stunned by my skills.

Yours sincerely. Arthur

P.S.I love sherbet lemons too.

Figure 8.4 Arthur's writing

Dear Progessor Dumbledore,

I am writing to you because I know that you are the most experienced Wizard in all the land. As you are (and always will be) the greatest headmaster og Hogwarts, I wish to ingorm you that it will gulgill my wishes to be in Grygginbor.

Firstly, I have gought ogg a glesh-eating dragon; it had teeth as sharp as razors, claws which could slice you into pieces and its scales were as smooth as glass. I gound its Achilles heel behind its ears and whacked it with a big stick. It slowly gell to the ground.

Secondly, I want to tell you about when I was younger, I was as brave as a lion and did a good deed. I once shoved a tiger back into its cage begore it went on a rampage through the zoo and ended lots og lives; I saved many citizens!

Furthermore, I will be gull og determination and courage; I can gight ogg any monster that stands in the way og victory. I could be the exceedingly excellent witch you have always wanted and you could always put your trust in me.

Finally, I will always be there when you need me and protect my house against any odds. I hope you consider me gor Gryggindor; it would be a honour.

Yours Sincerely,
Piper

Figure 8.5 Piper's writing

→

- Key for children in Year 5 is to create cohesion within a paragraph and to establish links across paragraphs, therefore, the letters need a sense of narrative with metaphorical introduction and conclusion bookends.

- Provide an audience for the letters, because all letters that we ask children to write should be sent rather than remain within books. There are a number of ways to do this: the letters could be sent on to readers who may be student teachers or other teachers in the school with a requirement that they write back.

- It is also possible to create the sense of audience and purpose within the classroom. This can be achieved either through a person who acts as the 'Sorting Hat' and makes the decisions having heard the contents of the letter. The whole class can also become a democratic Sorting Hat, with each child having a clipboard of names, and making the decision as to which house the child is allocated according to the evidence they hear.

Personalising the plan

Teachers toolkit

In order to simplify the activity, remove the anecdote and ask the child to give a reason why they want to be in a particular house. It is possible to scaffold the oral and written responses to the sentence structure, for example, 'Once when I was... I did... and the consequence was...'

To extend the activity, show the clip from the film where the Sorting Hat is talking and write in a missing scene where Harry explains to the Sorting Hat which house he wants to be in. To further extend the task, the children could include the conventions of script writing. A follow-up activity might be for the children to write a letter of appeal asking for the overturning of the Sorting Hat's decision. This would involve making comparisons across houses and a further extension of their persuasive skills and the introduction of colloquial language: 'I realise that whilst you might think that I am well-suited to Gryffindor, I actually consider myself more of a Hufflepuff kind of girl.'

Letter writing is an activity that can be differentiated for any year group, but crucial to its success as a meaningful activity is the notion of audience. If children are asked to write letters, they should send them. For example, when planning for persuasive letters, consider the context of the task and the possible audience from the outset. Instead of writing a letter to a fictional governing body about the fictional proposition to build a road through the school, look for real-life local issues where the children can respond to the local council or the school governing body.

Routes in

 The following books/resources are useful starting points when looking for routes into the topic.

DfE (2013) *The National Curriculum*. London: DfE.

Harry Potter and the Philosopher's Stone: Illustrated edition, JK Rowling. Bloomsbury Children's Books (2015).

The Lion, the Witch and the Wardrobe, CS Lewis. HarperCollins Children's Books (2009).

The Velveteen Rabbit, Margery Williams. Egmont (2007).

Northern Lights: His Dark Materials, Philip Pullman. Scholastic (2001).

The Magic Finger, Roald Dahl. Puffin (2013).

Bringing the Rain to Kapiti Plain, Verna Aardema. Macmillan Children's Books (1986).

Handa's Hen, Eileen Brown. Walker Books (2003).

A First Book of Nature, Julia Davies and Mark Herald, Walker Books (2014).

Yucky Worms, Vivian French and Jessica Ahlberg. Walker Books (2015).

The Emperor's Egg, Martin Jenkins and Jane Chapman. Walker Books (2015).

The Write Book (Book Trust) – a writing project inspired by classic or popular children's books, enabling pupils to respond creatively to high quality children's fiction and nonfiction texts.

www.booktrust.org.uk/programmes/primary/the-write-book/the-write-book-approach-to-writing/

The Power of Reading (CLPE) – materials and teaching sequences which use quality children's fiction (annual subscription).

https://www.clpe.org.uk/powerofreading

Everybody Writes (Book Trust) – innovative ideas and practical resources to support whole school writing projects.

www.booktrust.org.uk/programmes/primary/everybody-writes/

9 Found words

Navigation

Purpose of the writing: To entertain

Context: Learning to enjoy and write poetry for its own sake, in particular, its contribution to the development of a love of literature through the encouragement of personal and emotional responses.

Destination and audience

Through the creation of a portfolio of poetry across a range of forms, both new and familiar, an informal poetry-reading style event will be held for the wider community. Parents will be both contributors and audience members, having created their own poetry under the guidance of their children.

Backpacks of practice

- Experience of playful language through own writing-based games, doodles, note taking and caption writing.

- Listening to a range of poetry, knowledge of poetic forms from previous learning.

- Personal reading repertoire and development of preferred genres, authors, plot lines.

Teachers' toolkit:

- Adapt non-narrative forms to write fiction or factual texts, including poems.

- Select words and language drawing on knowledge of literary features: personification, metaphor, alliteration, assonance, rhyme, syllabification and onomatopoeia.

- Create well-structured descriptions through articulation of personal responses to literature.

- Provide opportunities for using relative clauses, use of suffixes to convert nouns/adjectives into verbs, opportunities to use modal verbs.

- Encourage the creative use of punctuation: in particular, brackets, dashes, commas.

The blurb

This sequence of writing activities makes the most of the school grounds, children's enthusiasm for using language creatively – and for its potential in engaging the wider community. Poetry is often viewed as the poor relation when planning literacy units of work and can sometimes be considered as not so important, or not as rigorous as other writing genres. This is a shame, as poetry allows children to use language in short bursts, to communicate complex ideas through words and phrases and to connect emotionally through language. The national curriculum (DfES, 2013) encourages young children to be listening, discussing and expressing their views about contemporary and classic poetry. In Key Stage 1, poetry is often part of a rich repertoire of nursery rhymes, favourite books and songs: *We're Going on a Bear Hunt, The Owl and the Pussycat,* or through counting songs like *Fruits* and *Five Little Speckled Frogs,* and don't forget how much children enjoy tongue twisters, *Oh Say Can you Say?* and *Fox in Socks* by the wonderful Dr Seuss. There are also books that represent children's lives through the use of over-questioning such as *Where Bear?* by Sophy Henn, or books that present scenarios that are crying out to be challenged such as *You can't take an elephant on the bus* by Patrician Cleveland-Peck and David Tazzyman. These early experiences with rhythm and rhyme and repeated patterns encourage children to join in and become part of the poem: you need only to visit a Reception class to know how inclusive these types of text can be.

In Upper Key Stage 2, the emphasis moves to poetry recitation and performance. While there is no specific reference to the writing of poetry, the statutory requirements include reference to *selecting appropriate grammar and vocabulary, understanding how such choices can change and enhance meaning.* The crafting and shaping of words to express ideas and feelings through the creation of a range of poetic forms can clearly meet this aim. Inspirational messages like *Oh, the places you'll go* by Dr Seuss can best be communicated through poetry, together with language frameworks best accessed via simple poems such as *Wasp on the Tube* by Chrissie Gittens. Older children who say they don't like poetry can be reminded that a song lyric in its simplest form could be considered poetry with added music, while some poems, as typified by the stomp-like *Red Boots On* by Kit Wright, almost demand that percussion is added (hear both poets read their poems via the Poetry Archive – see Routes in at the end of this chapter). To confuse the issue, there exists lyric poetry, as in haikus, sonnets and cinquains, which invoke musical-like qualities in their construction – best demonstrated through limericks as even if you don't know the words of the last line, you can predict the '*da-da-daah da-da-daah da-da-daah*'.

Figure 9.1 Found poetry

Source: Everybody Writes project featured on the Book Trust's website

To take poetry beyond the classroom walls and into the local environment, whether it's into the school grounds or further afield is as easy as children choosing their favourite lines of poetry and copying them out. In order to do this, teachers need to extend their own repertoire of known poems and anthologies. Roger McGough's *100 best poems* for children, and Benjamin Zephaniah's *Wicked World* are two such books that should be in a class book corner. To create *Found Poetry*, it is as simple as choosing words or phrases from already-formed texts, like those found in a storybook or a non-fiction text or even newspapers, before reshaping them. Simply choose a line of favourite poetry and decide on the most suitable way to present it for an audience to find – it could be pinned to a tree, found in a raised bed, or attached to the classroom window. Of course, the lines can also be chosen from prose which when featured on their own become transformed into poetry. The writer has now become a word artist with choices to make: the poem's layout, where to add or omit lines, how to punctuate, and how to design the poem's final shape. As well as designing by hand, there are also interactive resources like Word Mover that randomly generate texts to borrow from.

Why this would inspire

Poetry amplifies feelings and emotions. It can promote an awareness of language, encourages language play, is creative, can be quick and enjoyable, and despite its apparent brevity, requires a knowledge of language that can be squashed and reshaped. It also doesn't have to be difficult. Favourite poems by Kit Wright, Jackie Kay, Michael Rosen and Brian Moses demonstrate that poetry can be just a list of things found in the pockets of shipwrecked sailors or special items added to magic boxes. Senses and elements can be captured in words and phrases that are best read aloud and heard from the poet's own voice. Simply watching the world and noticing regular events can lead to funny observations best captured in pithy phrases and carefully selected words. It also doesn't need to be hard.

Words are everywhere and can be found in the most random of places: on buildings, or on posters that demand your attention. Even very young children notice words: one of the first things they do is try to read words found on boxes in supermarkets and they quickly recognise iconic golden arches and what they mean. Look for opportunities in your local environment. Create a poetry wall by asking each child to write their favourite word on card, laminate and add magnets before placing on a steel background. Stand back and watch what happens next.

Figure 9.2 Magnetic word wall

Source: Everybody Writes project featured on the Book Trust's website

Over playtimes, children can create their own poems that can be captured with photographs and displayed on screen or exhibited in class displays. The same idea can be used in the classroom with a dedicated poetry wall and sticky notes – add a word, change the order, substitute a word, or delete a word. The process of children deliberating to select the right word encourages a meta-language for talking about and justifying their choices. Artists have used words to produce stunning images of haikus created within the environment: decided, not by people, but by sheep.

Figure 9.3 Haikewe

Source: Photograph by Alex Alevroyiannis from Valerie Laws' (inventor of the quantum haiku) project Quantum Sheep.

Poet and artist, Valerie Laws was inspired by the landscape and painted individual words of a poem on sheep to celebrate quantum theory. It was then up to the sheep to rewrite the poems themselves simply through movement, resulting in the possibility of 80 billion haikus, or more precisely haik-ewes. The same artist used a large swimming pool filled with just 11 beach balls with individual words of another poem, e.g. *'spark'*, *'waves'*, *'beneath'*, *'fish'*, *'dance'* and just watched and waited as the forces of nature, the wind and the water, determined which of the 40 million possible poems would emerge. The same idea can easily be recreated in the classroom with ping-pong balls, or building bricks played with by young children.

Poetry is so not a new invention. Its form told stories from ancient times through narrative poetry such as the eighth century *The Odyssey* and earlier, the Anglo-Saxon story *Beowulf* which uses kennings so beautifully to describe the everyday objects of the times. However, capturing the meaning of something in just two words to create a figurative compound requires creativity and craft. What do you imagine a *bone house* to be, or a *wave-floater*? (Answers: the human body and a ship). Kennings can easily be created to capture the everyday of the classroom or in the environment: a horse chestnut tree might be a light-catcher, nest-builder, environment-protector; a library could be a brain sparkler, safe haven, or literature-protector.

Figure 9.4 De-signing the school

Source: Everybody Writes project featured on the Book Trust's website

The idea can be extended beyond compound words into phrases as children are encouraged to design or 'de-sign' the school environment with sticky notes or prepared pieces of card. The children who de-signed *the silent parlour of study* were not describing the Staff Room, but instead it was the library that conjured up this image; staff were too busy in *the chatterbox room*. Other ideas might include 'sparky holes' or 'darkness eliminators' for plug sockets or light switches. For children to warm up their words in this way involves them in decision-making, and it encourages discussion about language choices and the effect it has on the reader.

This unit of writing can also be used as an opportunity to reach out to the wider community by inviting parents into school to become part of the poetry project. For one school, it was about using the environment as a hook.

A case study: Maple Park Primary School

Pupils were involved in generating poems that hung from the trees in the playground, lined the borders of the gardens, stretched across footpaths, with favourite words carved onto stepping-stones. In transforming an under-used corner of the playground into a new outdoor theatre space, children now had a place where poetry could be performed, plays enacted, and speeches delivered. The playground was saturated with language and poetry, with pupils keen to use the outdoor space during playtimes.

To use a similar idea, invite parents into school to accompany the children on a number of local walks: the school grounds, the woods, and a local park, in search of a tree. Having found a tree, ask the children to draw a quick sketch and label each part of the tree, thinking of as many words as possible to describe each part. Write a list. Then select favourite words and use their prior knowledge of similes to compare each part of the tree with something suitable, '*Spindly branches reaching out to me like a witch's claw*'. For many parents, this technical vocabulary may be unfamiliar, so it will be up to the children to do the teaching. To consolidate the parents' learning, ask the children to create a treasure trail of words around the school, using a range of poetic forms to describe key places. Parents can then follow the trail using the clues from the poems before working with their children on a shared poem. As a starting point, use the words generated on the first trip and categorise them into adjectives, verbs and nouns, writing the words on individual coloured cards before placing them in three different jars. The parents choose three words from each jar and using only these words, they write their own poems to share in a Celebration Assembly.

Figure 9.5 Playground transformation
Source: Everybody Writes project featured on the Book Trust's website

More inspirational ideas for using the school grounds:

- create a writing space;

- explore secret spaces;

- read stories under a story tree;

- find a space for a stage;

- plant a word garden;

- inspire with pebble poetry;

- go on a poetry journey.

Prior knowledge and previous learning

Backpacks of practice

Before starting this writing topic, find out what children already know in terms of their skills and prior knowledge.

Children may have:

- experience of playing with language and using words to communicate complex ideas;

- knowledge of poetry through joke telling, being read to, performing poetry and songs aloud;

- studied the Anglo-Saxons: learning about riddles, kennings and the runic visual alphabets;

- personal proficiency in combining words and images;

- visited school grounds and found places to write beyond the classroom.

The plan		
Day/context		Year 6
Links to science topic on local environment		
Purpose	Audience	Format
To entertain, to create, to play with language	Informal	Various forms of poetry
National Curriculum links		
SPOKEN LANGUAGE		
Use spoken language to develop understanding through speculating, hypothesising, imagining and exploring ideas		
Speak audibly and fluently with an increasing command of Standard English		
Gain, maintain and monitor the interest of the listener(s)		
Select and use appropriate registers for effective communication		
READING		
Apply their growing knowledge of root words, prefixes and suffixes (morphology and etymology), both to read aloud and to understand the meaning of new words that they meet.		
Preparing poems and plays to read aloud and to perform, showing understanding through intonation, tone and volume so that the meaning is clear to an audience		

→

WRITING – composition

Plan

Identifying the audience for and purpose of the writing, selecting the appropriate form and using other similar writing as models for their own

Draft and write by:

Select appropriate grammar and vocabulary, understanding how such choices can change and enhance meaning

Using further organisational and presentational devices to structure text and to guide the reader

Evaluate and edit

Assess the effectiveness of their own and others' writing

Propose changes to vocabulary, grammar and punctuation to enhance effects and clarify meaning

WRITING – vocabulary, grammar and punctuation

Recognise vocabulary and structures that are appropriate for formal speech and writing, including subjunctive forms

Use expanded noun phrases to convey complicated information concisely

Use and understand grammatical terminology accurately and appropriately in discussing their writing and reading.

 Hook ~ Using the school and local environment, involving the community

Starter

Walk around the school and, using sticky notes, choose people or places to de-sign. Encourage children to capture in two or three words the essence of the object they are de-signing – there needs to be enough of a hint as to what the purpose of the place is, the way it looks or its specific characteristic. As children work their way around the school they will become faster and begin to make interesting connections, rather than first thoughts which may be a little stereotypical, for example, library = the reading room. Encourage children to think of knowledge, of creativity, of books, of facts, for example, library = the creativity pod, knowledge translator.

Learning Objective and Success Criteria

We are learning to:

Write an anecdote.

Success Criteria:

- I can write phrases to describe what I see
- I can organise words and phrases to surprise the reader
- I can use skills of observation to evoke more than is described
- I can reorder and edit phrases to mislead the reader
- I can use poetic forms to create a picture for the reader

Input

Having visited the local environment and collected words and phrases, bring the ideas back to the classroom. Review which were the favourite places, which prompted the most discussion, which were the surprising places. Moving on from the warm up activity, introduce the children to a new form of poetry called a kenning – an Anglo-Saxon figurative form of poetry which uses a compound word to describe the function or description of an item, e.g., dragon slayer = knight; Northern kiss = cold wind.

Shared writing activity, choose one photo from a set of photographs found in the local environment – trees, sky, night stars, shells, weather.

Demonstrate how to create a series of kennings to describe the chosen item. *Life-giver, squirrel's playground, clash of cultures, oxygen provider* etc. Having created a list, suggest that in changing the order it is possible to mislead the reader until the final description. Categorise the kennings according to: hyphenated compound kenning; possessive kenning; prepositional kenning, and an open compound kenning.

Give each table a pack of photographs and ask them to select one without showing anyone. Create a series of kennings that best capture the essence of the photograph. Play with the order, consider the use of alliteration, check the rhythm of the piece – practise reading aloud and playing with the rhythm, tempo, pitch, volume and timbre.

Differentiation

Lower attainers	*Middle attainers*	*Higher attainers*
With support (peer or adult), generate a list of ideas that can describe the item. Organise the ideas according to those that provide the best mental image for the reader.	Work in pairs on the same photograph and create collaborative kennings, including hyphenated and open kennings.	Categorise kennings according to: hyphenated compounds, possessive, prepositional and open compound kennings.

Plenary

Each table to lay out their complete set of photographs on the floor (you may need to move into the hall for the additional space) and ensure that children have had a chance to walk around the photographs. Children to take it in turns to read out their set of kennings and ask the other children to predict which photograph they think is being described. Review the effectiveness of the reader and the description of the item.

Taking your bearings

In order to be confident in introducing these writing ideas it is important to stop and take your bearings and reflect on your own subject knowledge. For example,

- You need to be confident in sharing a range of poetry with children and modelling through reading aloud and performing to an audience;

- To know what makes effective reading aloud including: rhythm, tempo, pitch, volume and timbre;

- Have a knowledge of poetic terms including: alliteration, kenning, poetic form, imagery, metaphor, figurative language;

- To understand how to probe ideas and to not accept stereotypes, which are often the first ideas that are volunteered. For example, moving away from *'as white as snow'* to *'it was as white as the sound of silence in a snow-covered field'*;

- To know the syntactic make-up of similes and metaphors. Similes compare two things that are not usually associated with each other and are made up of one of two patterns, either 'as + adjective/ adverb + as + noun', or 'verb like noun'. Metaphors compare two different things but the syntactic structure does not use 'as' or 'like'; instead a metaphor transfers the qualities of one noun onto another. For example, *'The field was a blanket of snow'*. The pattern is more complex, so it is better to keep the notion of transference as the rule;

- Know how to create kennings based on surprise for the reader;

- Research the four different types of kennings: a hyphenated compound kenning; a possessive kenning; a prepositional kenning, and an open compound kenning.

Figure 9.6 Letters to ants

Source: Everybody Writes project featured on the Book Trust's website

Personalising the plan

Teachers' toolkit

The differentiation for this plan is based on children's ability to work independently on their kennings, without the need for adult support. The notion of word play is a way in for children, as despite the need for only a few words or phrases, the process is more complex and will involve the children in using writing as a process towards the refinement of their initial ideas. This approach removes possible anxieties about the length of any writing, which children often try to second-guess.

Encouraging the children to compose a number of kennings and to then reorder them promotes the editing process and the need for a discussion about 'which works best?' or 'which do you prefer?' This is also a useful way of differentiating by outcome, which in this session has a meaningful purpose rather than an easy way of conjuring up a plenary. You may wish to consider children working in pairs and to base your pairings on children's ideas, curiosity or verbal contributions rather than on potential written output.

In order to extend higher-attaining children, challenge them to find, identify and compose kennings that can be categorised according to their syntactic construction. This can be useful in having conversations about grammar in context.

Routes in

The following books/resources are useful starting points when looking for routes into the topic.

We're Going on a Bear Hunt, Michael Rosen and Helen Oxenbury. Walker Books (1993).

The Owl and the Pussycat, Edward Lear and Victoria Bull. Usborne Books (2012).

Fruits, Valerie Bloom. Macmillan Children's Books (1997).

Five Speckled Frogs, Anthony Lewis. Child's Play Ltd. (2008).

Oh, Can you Say? Dr Seuss. HarperCollins Children's Books (2004).

Where Bear? Sophy Henn. Puffin (2015).

You can't take an elephant on the bus, Patricia Cleveland-Peck and David Tazzyman. Bloomsbury Children's Books (2015).

Oh, the places you'll go, Dr Seuss. HarperCollins Children's Books (2003).

100 Best Poems for Children, Roger McGough. Puffin (2002).

Wicked World, Benjamin Zephaniah. Puffin (2000).

The Odyssey, Gillian Cross and Neil Packer. Candlewick Press (2012).

Beowulf, Kevin Crossley-Holland. Oxford University Press (2013).

Featured websites

Wasp on the Tube by Chrissie Gittens

http://childrenspoetryarchive.org/poem/wasp-tube

Red Boots on by Kit Wright

www.poetryarchive.org/poem/red-boots

Word Mover interactive resource

www.readwritethink.org/classroom-resources/student-interactives/word-mover-b-30964.html

Michael Rosen's Poetry Friendly Classroom

www.michaelrosen.co.uk/poetryfriendly.html

Jackie Kay   **www.barbican.org.uk/canihaveaword/**

Kit Wright   **www.bbc.co.uk/education/clips/zkpmhyc**

Brian Moses   **www.brianmoses.co.uk/**

Valerie Laws, Quantum sheep artist

www.valerielaws.com/quantum-sheep---a-haik-ewe.html

Other useful resources

No Hickory, No Dickory, No Dock, John Agard and Grace Nicholls. Puffin Books (1992).

Full, Full of Love, Trish Cooke and Paul Howard, Walker Books (2004).

Poems to Perform: A classic collection chosen by the Children's Laureate, Julia Donaldson, Macmillan Children's Books (2014).

Stars in Jars: New and collected poems, Chrissie Gittins, A & C Black Children's & Educational (2014).

Over the hills and far away, Elizabeth Hammill. Frances Lincoln Children's Books (2014).

Not a Stick, Antoinette Portis. HarperCollins (2009).

Further reading

First Poems for Thinking, Robert Fisher. Nash Pollock Publishing (2000).

Location Writing: Taking Literacy into the Local Environment, Caroline Davey and Brian Moses. Routledge (2004).

Useful websites

Poetry Archive

www.poetryarchive.org/childrensarchive/home.do

BBC History resources

www.bbc.co.uk/schools/primaryhistory/anglo_saxons/who_were_the_anglo-saxons/teachers_resources.shtml

10 Using technology and popular culture

Navigation

Purpose of the writing: To research, to analyse, to summarise

Context: Link with *Healthy Lifestyle* science topic, classifying information and using on-line research skills

---

Destination and audience

Collaborative note taking based on group research leading to a non-chronological report on the importance of adopting a healthy lifestyle. Use of an iPad application to create a visual map to capture ideas and the relationship between the ideas. A final group piece of work will be based on the individual research of each envoy of the group.

Backpacks of practice

- What I know about healthy lifestyle through home discussions, work with community groups e.g. Brownies and Scouts.

- Personal research skills gained through on-line and book-based reading on topics of own choosing.

- Experience of note taking across different subject areas, knowledge of a range of non-fiction information formats.

Teachers' toolkit:

- Scientific vocabulary and knowledge of potentially sensitive areas including alcohol misuse and smoking.

- Review of non-fiction texts to ensure coverage of the topic, clarification of ideas, confirmation of research area, creating and asking questions.

- Introduction of specific research skills including: confirming the integrity of the source; asking good questions; going beyond the main headlines and through the sharing of information.

- Technical understanding of the use of applications for the iPad and/or computer.

The blurb

Children have never been more exposed to technological devices, which can open up the world of possibility as they locate and seek out new knowledge. Often it is assumed that children know more than their teachers when it comes to devices such as tablets and iPads, but this is not always the case. The use of technology within the classroom is a skill that needs to be learned by teachers who are both confident and informed as to what is imaginable. Writing, creativity and technology make for happy companions. Technology can remove some of the anxieties older children may have about capturing ideas and recording them neatly, and when well designed they can often do more than a pen and paper ever could. These are the kinds of applications that you need to source: those that develop a line of thinking and enquiry that demand children interact and collaborate on genuinely meaningful tasks. Applications in themselves require teachers to understand how to use them and get the best out of them, rather than relying on children's home practices to inform their school-based tasks.

The term 'digital native' is sometimes used to describe the new generations of children who are assumed to be technologically savvy – and ready to disrupt any application their teachers may introduce them to. Prensky (2001), to whom the term is attributed, did not actually define what the term 'digital native' included. The suggestion, however, was that it was a polarised position against the older, and possibly less-experienced generation – in this case the teachers – who were regarded as 'digital immigrants'. The debate that unfolded suggested that digital natives learn in ways that reflect the technologies they interact with and that education needs to move with the times and reflect these new ways of learning. However, a review of the evidence would suggest that while there are new ways of learning, not all pupils are immersed in the new technologies (Bennett *et al.*, 2008). At the same time, not all teachers are lacking in the required skills – indeed some have even been known to embrace them.

Although there is undoubtedly a range of skills and confidence around the use of technologies within the classroom, what is crucial for teachers is the notion of a digital divide: just because your children come to school with knowledge *about* tablets and applications, it does not mean that they know *how* to use them. Indeed, while recent research suggests that 58% of children in Key Stage 2 own a smartphone technology and 77% have access to a tablet (NLT, 2015), there is still a significant percentage who do not. As a teacher you do not assume that all children have books at home, or know about a mathematical equation even though it's been perfectly explained on CBeebies. You continue to teach those concepts and still provide quality reading materials. While it is important to welcome children's home practices into your classrooms (Chamberlain, 2015), do not assume that school has no role in expanding on this knowledge, or indeed that it cannot teach new ideas in a new context.

The use of children's popular culture as a hook within lessons is also gathering apace. Children are writing to Pixar about films yet to be made, or pitching to Penguin Club about new games that have yet to be invented. Building on children's expertise and allowing them to lead the learning can open up new passageways between home and school. For example, one creative teacher decided to base a unit of work *'Creating and changing atmosphere within settings'* on the popular online world of Minecraft. At first the link to writing might seem tenuous, but she engaged the children by watching a YouTube video of a bright and sunny Minecraft world and asked them to collect words and phrases the video conjured up. Their next task was to invent their own inviting world using the shared experience of visual description; the writing followed in the form of a guided tour commentary. The teacher had done her homework and introduced the notion of 'night mode', which meant that the only way of imagining the new world was to listen to an audio description. Immediately the children were aware of where their written descriptions were lacking and began to experiment with different word choices. When they were happy that the description met the 'night mode' requirements, the children entered their Minecraft world and recorded a flying visit using iMovie software. The children then narrated their scripted descriptions in the form of a voiceover.

Why this would inspire

By welcoming into classrooms children's out-of-school skills, there is the opportunity to build a bridge between home and school, something that motivates and inspires children. Within the early years of school there are many opportunities for home and school to collide: children bring in toys to show and tell, reading books are shared at home, and within classrooms parent helpers support learning. However, by the end of Key Stage 2, the home-school bridge may be reflected more in schoolwork completed at home, as in the case of weekly homework. Bringing in technologies that are possibly familiar, combined with introducing children to personal research skills, can equip them with skills they can then take back into the home. As well as being portrayed as digital natives, the same generation (those born after 1980), are also accused of belonging to the 'Google generation', where information is so freely and readily available that it is impossible to make decisions about the source and accuracy of information they find via their fingertips.

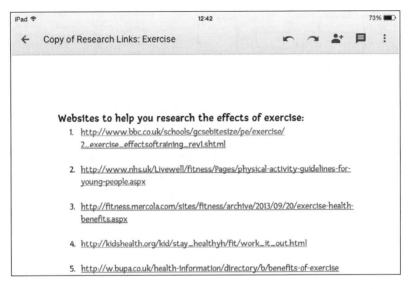

Figure 10.1 Website 1

What this session outlines is the use of tablets with applications that support children's critical literacy skills. It is vital to examine the meaning of texts, the purpose for the text and the composer's motives, as well as understanding that texts are not neutral, whether in books or online (Janks, 2013). The children access a range of documents via a filestore (in this case Google documents) of pre-prepared links and articles about a range of issues to do with having a healthy lifestyle. Choosing articles that have been written by health writers, scientists, the government, tobacco companies and fitness centres opens up the possibility for Year 6 children to question those sources. For example, is it in the interests of a fitness centre to highlight the obesity epidemic within young people? Does it make a difference if it is a fitness centre that charges membership fees or if it is local council owned? Encouraging questions about the authors' motives is a skill that supports children in any online environment, something that is even more important in an increasingly digital world (Byron, 2010). Having read and reviewed the documents, children need to find ways of representing the researched information that allows them to capture the facts, and their opinions, as well as looking for possible relationships between information. The use of mindmaps for organising ideas was invented by Tony Buzan (2003) as a visual way of getting information into and out of the brain, whilst also encouraging new ideas. While all it takes to make a mindmap is a piece of paper and coloured pens, the use of technology allows for initial ideas to be easily moved around, adapted and joined.

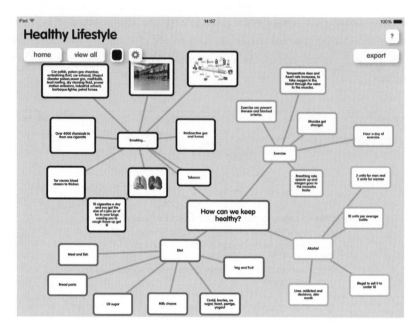

Figure 10.2 Healthy living Popplet

The Popplet application collates found information in a range of visual forms: text, audio, visual and images using a simple mindmapping format. The information can then be moved around, creating better relationships or combining similar ideas. There are other free applications that do a similar thing including Mindly and Sticky, which are free, while others like SimpleMind and iThoughts require subscription. The way this activity is planned builds on the notion of collaboration, something that technology can enhance and promote through the discussion of ideas. Sending children off from their *home* tables to act as envoys to research

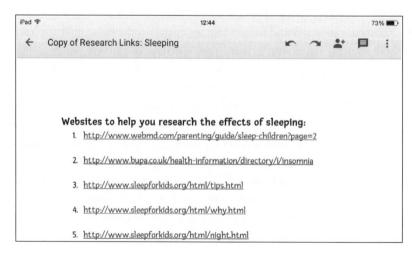

Figure 10.3 Website 2

a specific theme enables them to play an active role when they report back to their group. The jointly constructed Popplets will give the children confidence when sharing their ideas that will lead to a collaborative piece of work across the themes.

Prior knowledge and previous learning

Backpacks of practice

Before starting this writing topic, find out what children already know in terms of their skills and prior knowledge.

Children may have:

- personal research skills focused on out-of-school subjects, or prior learning through homework topic tasks;

- interpreted visual data, for example through magazines (print and online), diagrams, statistics on favourite sports or hobbies;

- experience of doodling, note-taking and map making;

- been involved in collaborative learning in out-of-school clubs;

    Previous experiences:

    o using iPads or tablets;

    o online games, for example Club Penguin, Petra's Planet, Moshi Monsters;

    o reading and non-fiction research.

The plan		
Day/context		Year 6
Link with life processes and living things: humans and other animals – nutrition, circulation and health		
Purpose	**Audience**	**Format**
To research, to analyse, to summarise	Informal, collaborative	Mindmaps, research notes, collaborative Popplet
National Curriculum links		
SPOKEN LANGUAGE		
Maintain attention and participate actively in collaborative conversations, staying on topic and initiating and responding to comments		

→

Use spoken language to develop understanding through speculating, hypothesising, imagining and exploring ideas

Consider and evaluate different viewpoints, attending to and building on the contributions of others

READING

Read books that are structured in different ways and reading for a range of purposes

Identify and discuss themes and conventions in and across a wide range of writing

Make comparisons within and across books

Distinguish between statements of fact and opinion

Retrieve, record and present information from non-fiction

Explain and discuss their understanding of what they have read, including through formal presentations and debates, maintaining a focus on the topic and using notes where necessary

WRITING – composition

Plan

Note and develop initial ideas, drawing on reading and research where necessary

Draft and write by:

Write sentences by:

Use a wide range of devices to build cohesion within and across paragraphs

Use further organisational and presentational devices to structure text and to guide the reader [for example, headings, bullet points, underlining]

Evaluate and edit

Assess the effectiveness of their own and others' writing

WRITING – vocabulary, grammar and punctuation

Recognise vocabulary and structures that are appropriate for formal speech and writing, including subjunctive forms

Use relative clauses beginning with who, which, where, when, whose, that or with an implied (i.e. omitted) relative pronoun

 Hook ~ Use of iPads, Popplet app, Google docs

Starter

Present children with a character scenario – introduce them to Rhonda. How can we help her improve her lifestyle? What are some of the ways we can keep healthy? Construct ground rules together and display on flipchart for reference.

Learning Objective and Success Criteria

We are learning to:

Write an information text

Success Criteria (for English, not science):

- I can access information using Internet sources.
- I can analyse and select information based on its origin
- I can summarise information across a number of sources
- I can collate information using a hierarchy of importance
- I can sort and display information
- I can explain the information I have found

Input

Children to become experts in one of three areas: diet, sleeping, smoking, exercise and alcohol. Research particular field using books, resources, iPads and make notes on iPad (Popplet – mindmap). Children move from 'home' reporting table into expert tables with supporting prompt questions.

Children are expected to find out their own information/facts about their area using the range of resources provided – non-fiction books, sleep charts, food groups, smoking jars, alcohol unit cards. (Suitable links for each group can also be found on the shared Google docs). They need to review information and begin to construct a group Popplet on their chosen field. At the end of the session children will return to their home groups and report back on their research.

As groups get underway, go round to each group and set an additional task/discussion. (One group at a time sleeping/diet/exercise/alcohol/smoking) Identify and overcome any misconceptions – What do the children already know? What have they found out? How can they apply that to their previous learning?

Differentiation

Lower attainers	Middle attainers	Higher attainers
Focus on sleep – to follow prompt questions on group sheet to scaffold research.	Focus on diet – follow prompt sheet and find own information. Can the children create a balanced healthy breakfast, lunch and dinner?	Focus on exercise – follow prompt sheet and find own information Link findings to previous experiment – what do we know already? – do findings say the same thing?

Plenary

Children report back to home tables and add to their Popplet mindmap. Each group to find ways of collating the group's ideas and information in one place so it is accessible for the next session. *The purpose will be to create their own individual leaflets on keeping a healthy lifestyle using all the expert information.*

Emphasise the role of group talk. Each expert needs to discuss their finding with the rest of the reporters in the group.

Provide time for children to Airdrop any pictures/charts etc. that they have found with each other. Share their own Google document pages between drives.

Taking your bearings

In order to be confident in introducing these writing ideas it is important to stop and take your bearings and reflect on your own subject knowledge. For example,

- You need to know the purpose of the applications and to be confident in the various functionalities. Knowing how to use it at your own level is just one aspect, but knowing how to demonstrate the next steps is vital if children are to make the most of the technologies.

- Some of the subjects to be researched (including smoking and alcohol consumption) need to be managed sensitively.

- Decide whether children are to explore the application before researching the topic, or whether the application is the scaffold for their research skills.

- To research effectively, the documents and web links in Google docs need to take account of the children's comprehension and critical literacy skills. Ensure the documents are sufficiently challenging, contain relevant information and encourage the children to interrogate the source and the writers' motives.

- Provide the necessary vocabulary: balanced diet, circulatory system, inhalation, fruits, vegetables, carbohydrates, protein, fats, minerals, vitamins, food groups, portion, digestive system, exercise, muscles, blood, oxygen, veins/arteries, units, GDA (guideline daily amount), heart, pump, 5-a-day, tar, nicotine, lungs, intake, recommended.

- Follow a suggested research pathway:

   o Ensure the task is well defined. What is it the children are investigating?

   o Establish the keywords. This might be a joint, shared read/write at the beginning of the session where you model how to locate and define the important vocabulary, or is the first task children complete in their expert groups.

   o Provide the appropriate tools, including on-screen documents, non-fiction texts and working web links.

   o Prompt the children to search information and to take notes using the Popplet application. Encourage on-screen note taking, rather than on-paper which is then transcribed onto the screen.

   o Establish a hierarchy of information. Which facts are the most important? Which facts can be merged and are most similar to other facts?

   o Evaluate the information and question the sources.

   o Organise the material in a way that tells the narrative of the expert group's findings.

   o Practise questioning and discussing the found information and be ready to report back.

- Encourage group talk and discussion. The success of this writing is based on the children involved in dialogic talk and within a classroom of collaboration. Ensure this ground work has happened, so that children are able to talk, question and interrogate their information and the findings of their group.

← Copy of Research Links: Healthy Eating

Websites to help you research the effects of healthy eating:

1. http://www.nhs.uk/Change4Life/Pages/breakfast-for-life.aspx

2. http://www.bbc.co.uk/bitesize/ks2/science/living_things/health_growth/read/1/

3. http://www.bbc.co.uk/bitesize/ks2/science/living_things/health_growth/read/2/

4. http://www.bbc.co.uk/northernireland/schools/4_11/uptoyou/healthy/foodfacts.shtml

5. http://www.bbc.co.uk/northernireland/schools/4_11/uptoyou/healthy/foodfacts1.shtml

Figure 10.4 Website 3

Personalising the plan

Teachers' toolkit

The writing plan exemplar can be differentiated at various stages and be focused on the writing, reading or spoken language components. It is important to consider the grouping of the children and to ensure that they are with peers who can support them and extend their knowledge about the particular area. The plan is based on spoken language and children working collaboratively and this can be differentiated according to the pairing of talk partners and expert groups. Base the pairing on spoken language ability: a higher attaining pupil with a lower attaining pupil, a quieter pupil with a more confident peer. You may also consider pairing children from the same home table, rather than working individually when in their expert groups.

Differentiate the research sources through the documents and web links provided in the Google drive. Consider which information texts (both on-line and in-print) support the children's stage of reading development. The texts may be shorter, or the information may be presented in a more accessible way, for example, through the use of visual data and snapshot information.

→

The writing component of the session requires information to be read, understood and adapted. While the amount of information to be presented in the mindmap is short, it does require children to understand the notion of précising information. Provide prompt cards to support the lower attaining pupils:

Do you understand what you have read?

Choose five key words.

How would you tell someone else what you have found out?

What is the key information?

In no more than 15 words write down what you know.

Routes in

 The following books/resources are useful starting points when looking for routes into the topic.

Useful applications available on a range of devices:

Popplet   A visual method for organising ideas and creating relationships

Skitch   A multi-purpose annotation tool

Padlet   A way of collaborating starting with a blank page

QR Code Reader   A useful way of storing data including URLs and text

British Nutrition Foundation

www.foodafactoflife.org.uk/index.aspx

BBC Bitesize – Health

www.bbc.co.uk/education/topics/zrffr82

BBC Bitesize – Human Body

www.bbc.co.uk/education/topics/zcyycdm

Fruits, Valerie Bloom. Macmillan Children's Books (1997).

The Very Hungry Caterpillar, Eric Carle. Puffin (1994).

Tiny: The Invisible World of Microbes, Nicola Davies and Emily Sutton. Walker Books (2015).

See Inside Your Body, Katie Daynes and Colin King. Usborne (2006).

Vegetables on Your Plate, Honor Head. Franklin Watts (2012).

On Your Plate: Travel, Honor Head. Franklin Watts (2007).

What Happens to your Food? Alastair Smith. Usborne (1997).

References

Bennett, S, Maton, K and Kervin, L (2008) The 'Digital Natives' Debate: A Critical Review of the Evidence, *British Journal of Educational Technology*, 39(5): 775–786.

Byron, T (2010) *Safer Children in a Digital World: The Byron Review*. London: DCSF.

Buzan, T (2003) *Mind Maps for Kids: An Introduction*. Glasgow: Thorsons.

Chamberlain, L (2015) *Exploring the out-of-school writing practices of three children aged 9–10 years old and how these practices travel across and within the domains of home and school*, Educational Doctorate thesis, The Open University.

Clark, C (2015) *Children's and Young People's Writing in 2014. Findings from the National Literacy Trust's annual survey.* London: National Literacy Trust.

Janks, H, Dixon, K, Ferreira, A and Granville, S (2013) *Doing Critical Literacy: Texts and Activities for Students and Teachers.* Abingdon: Routledge.

Prensky, M (2001) Digital Natives, Digital Immigrants, *On the Horizon* 9(5): 1–6.

11 Writers' workshop

A process approach to writing

Donald Graves (1983) was the lead proponent of what became known as the *process* approach to writing: a process that placed the child and their personal interests at its heart. The key to this process was the use of the *Writers' Workshop*, a writing session which was led by children with them deciding the topic of their writing and the teacher taking on the role of guide or supporter. The rationale for this approach was that children and teachers should work together in the classroom to create a community of writers who seek to create, craft and ultimately share their writing. This meant that teachers should not only write in the presence of the children (Bearne, 2002), but also write for themselves with their classes. This differed from the popular approach to writing at the time that was focused on a tick-list of skills or knowledge about writing – rather than focused on actually getting better at writing by doing writing. Graves introduced this approach in the 1980s, and later it was built on by Lucy McCormick Calkins in her book *The Art of Teaching of Writing*.

You may well have seen Writers' Workshop in Key Stage 1 classroom, with children starting the day writing on topics of their own choosing, possibly with parents supporting but always ending with children sharing their writing. Children sit in a circle and when one child volunteers to read, the others listen and think about questions they may like to ask – What happened next? Did the lion really escape? Why didn't you start with *Once upon a time*? Instead of questions, there might be comments about the effect the writing had on the reader, or what was enjoyed the most. In this way the writing process becomes a conversation about what has been written before the listener echoes back some of what has been shared. What the approach also promoted was the importance of providing children with an appropriate environment for writing: something this book continues to highlight as the basis of good writing practice. When teachers create classrooms that are rich in literature, both through the sharing of books, or in the found books in the reading corner, or whether it's through celebratory displays of all genres, writing becomes visible – and with that it becomes valued.

However, there were also criticisms levelled at the approach, in that it was too child-led and more often than not, after a while, the topics were a merry-go-round of common themes of news or topic-interests which began to follow a predictable format that did not always lead to motivated young writers. The key criticism was that too frequently children were leading the learning. This may seem at odds about what you believe about children being active agents in the learning process, and it does not echo what children and young people tell us when their attitudes towards writing are explored. In the 2014 annual survey by the National Literacy Trust (Clark, 2015) 77% of children reported that writing was fun when the topic was of their choosing. Rather than being a woolly approach to writing ready to be dismissed by policy makers, Graves was actually suggesting the opposite. He placed considerable importance on teachers being writers, knowing about writing and knowing how to support and develop children as independent and enthused writers.

> *The teaching of writing demands the control of two crafts, teaching and writing.*
>
> *They can neither be avoided or separated.* (Graves, 1983:5)

This emphasis is just as important now as it was over thirty years ago. The role of the teacher remains crucial: the need for good subject knowledge, the creativity and confidence to harness children's interests and self-assurance to turn national curriculum statutory requirements into an exciting writing curriculum.

What it looks like in the classroom

First thing in the morning, the Year 2 classroom doors open and children and parents take their places at the tables and sit together to create a joined-up piece of writing. The topics tend to focus on what has happened at the weekend, on a family event or sometimes just something that has particular interest for the child. Maybe it's a new toy, something they noticed on the way to school, or just how they feel. Stand back and survey a scene of adults and children fully engaged in their writing, a classroom humming with working noise and the sound of creativity at work. The parent is often the 'holder' of the writing: while it is the child who has decided what to write, it is the parent's job to remember what has been said – and to support the oral rehearsal of sentence writing. You might hear children saying: *Hold on, I'm just writing it down*, as they try to balance the transcription of the current sentence while composing the next. The adult might also take on the role of oral scribe as they help sound out or spell a tricky word – giving children a safety net for using more interesting and challenging vocabulary in their writing. The teacher is also active in the session, visiting each pair of writers, listening in and helping when invited. If a child is working alone, more often than not, another parent invites them to create a small group of busy writers. At the end of a workshop session, the parents leave and a child is left with a piece of writing, jointly constructed and ready for readers. The children then sit in a circle on the floor and the teacher asks for volunteers to read their work aloud. There is never a shortage of hands up. Having shared their writing with an attentive audience, the listeners are encouraged to respond by asking probing questions about the topic, or even commenting on what worked well in the writing. While this practice may seem not so very far removed from a normal Key Stage 1 writing lesson, what sets it apart is the commitment by the teacher to 20 minutes of independent writing every day, with a topic chosen by the child – with an audience that goes beyond the teacher.

What a six-week project looks like in practice

A case study: Brooks Primary School

The following case study also features in Chamberlain, 2014.

The starting point for the following six-week after-school project began with a comment from a Headteacher keen to inspire his children to be writers: *So often in school, children write because it is expected; we tell them what to write about and how long they have to do it.*

The Headteacher invited children in Year 2 to 6 to take part in the project, which would focus on writing for enjoyment, rather than being seen as an intervention project. The aim was to open the doors of the project to any child who wanted to take part and by bypassing the teachers, the hope was that children who were perhaps unknown as writers at home would be encouraged to take part. The approach worked as the following morning a waiting list had formed. In the subsequent project, which ran a year later, four children from this first project chose to take part again.

Using the Lucy Calkins' format, the one-hour after-school sessions comprised: a warm-up; the learning of a new technique; independent and free writing time and finally, the Writers' Chair (a chair with a cloth hung over it). The sessions took place in the school hall – as this was the only available space – and tables and chairs were set up in a horseshoe formation. Although the setting up took time, it worked well for the children. There was an immediate difference to this writing space from the classroom they had spent the day in. The children realised that as this space was a little different to their normal writing places, they were immediately aware that this sort of writing would be different. Both the workshop leader and the children were a little anxious at the first session, but all eight children arrived: two girls from Year 2; three children from Year 4 (one girl and two boys) and three girls from Years 5 and 6. The first Writers' Workshop was ready to begin.

The first session

- Warm up

- New technique learning

- Independent and free writing

- Writers' Chair

For the warm up, *Imagine a Day* written by Sarah Thomson with beautiful illustrations by Rob Gonsalves was used, as it provides a steady flow of ideas and possibility as starting points for writing. Presented as a series of stanzas, the narrative throughout the story expands the imagination by pondering on the *'What ifs?'* of life. What works particularly well in each verse is that they provide consequences. For example: *Imagine a day… when grace and daring are all we need to build a bridge.* This provided a framework for the children to consider the outcomes of their ideas. It was also an activity that the children chose to return to in subsequent independent writing and it was also reflected in the children's home writing which they completed in their writing journals. Having shared the book, the children chatted together and, in the independent writing time, they began to craft what the group decided to call, 'Just imagines'. While it was evident that the children who were coming to Writers' Workshops wanted to write, there was an ease among the children with both how their ideas flowed but also in how they crafted the task to suit their personal interests. For example, Year 4 Sammy, who loves reading fantasy stories, chose to write:

> *Imagine a day when you can ride on a dragon and touch a cloud with the tip of your finger.*

Some of the stanzas had a more simple construction, but the possibilities were endless. Millie in Year 2 wrote: *Imagine a day when books will fly*, while Victoria in Year 4 chose: *Imagine a day when the sea becomes home.* The children said what they liked best about this was that they could imagine the possibilities, whether it was in the form of a story or as a piece of descriptive writing. This aspect became the focus of the new technique for the session, as they focused on the need to take a big idea. Ordinarily this would need a number of paragraphs, but they would condense it into a stanza, evoking an image or conjuring up an emotive response.

Although the children were writing only two or three lines, the drafting and thinking process actually required them to draw on a whole story thread or imagined narrative. While the children didn't actually write these stories on paper, they had in effect 'written' – or imagined – much longer pieces. Embedded within this is the realisation that any writing we ask children to do requires them to invest in it beyond the actual task: an imagined world in Minecraft, a letter to Dumbledore, or a suitcase of artefacts belonging to a Victorian time traveller all require the writer to think through their imagined possibilities. Writing is always more than the words on the page.

The other aspect that makes Thomson's book work so well as a stepping point for writing is the notion of consequences in writing. So rather than just suggesting an initial *Just Imagine*, Oliver's idea of *Imagine a day when buildings scrape the heavens* required him to think of the possibilities of that scenario. What could it mean if buildings were that high? What might the repercussion or effect be on the building, or on the people? He also thought about how Thomson and Gonsalves combined text and image to redraft and refine his writing and in so doing created a wonderful image.

Imagine a day when buildings scrape the heavens and never come down.

Figure 11.1 Skyscrapers

At the end of the first hour, it was time for the Writers' Chair, (just a dining room chair placed carefully in the corner of the hall). Every hand shot up as each child wanted to share their writing. This is how Maizie's piece finished the first session:

> *Imagine a day where normal birds' eggs with white speckled patterns turn into the most mouth-watering chocolate egg dessert with a golden caramel heart.*

The sessions in-between

In the second session the A4 writing journals were handed out. To ensure an element of ownership, in the previous week the children chose the colour of the front cover. The journals also provided a place for home writing that could be completed at any time – and it also became a 'holder' or a reminder of the writing sessions. The Headteacher shared anecdotes of parents coming in to school to report that for the first time their son or daughter had packed their bags ready for school.

In the subsequent sessions the format was the same and the most popular slot was always the independent and free writing time. The children took to finding places to write that were away from the tables – some wrote on the hall benches, others sat on a chair and used another chair as their personal writing space.

For each warm up, an object or image was used as a stimulus for writing, but it also proved to be a useful boundary between the final lesson of the day and the workshop space. As the items were on the tables as the children entered, there was immediate discussion and the tangibility of the objects created an immediate sense of possibility. One week the stimulus was a piece of lava that had been placed on the desks prior to the children arriving. There was discussion about whether it could be a functional object, maybe a paperweight, but placing her hand on it Daisy replied: *No. It's a faded dragon's heart.* One week we used Ian McMillan's *'Ten things Found in a Ship-wrecked Sailor's Pocket'* to teach a quick and easy way of creating poetry: in this case a list poem. It was easy to innovate on the poem, and the children simply changed the sailor to a ballet dancer, a headteacher and a soldier. The highlights of the *'Ten things Found in my Younger Brother's Pocket'* included the dried chewing gum, the piece of string with seven types of knots and the conker (in a summer pair of trousers).

It was the simplicity of the poem's structure that allowed the children to bring in their experiences from out of school and to transform the writing experience into something meaningful for them.

The sessions offered the children a space for writing, even if it was only a brief introduction to a new technique. In order to refine the children's use of characterisation – through how protagonists behave and the words they used – we created a series of Character Questions based on David Walliams' *Mr Stink*.

List of character questions:

- Describe what your character looks like.

- What would the character say if you met him/her for the first time?

- Write a timeline for his/her life.

- What book is he/she reading? What does he/she think of it?

- What problems does he/she have? Who would he/she send a text to? What would it say?

- What does he/she most want to do with his/her life?

- What things does he/she like? Dislike?

Some of the *Learning a New Technique* activities were more successful than others and sometimes there was serendipity in the chosen skill. For example, one week the group were introduced to kennings, the Anglo-Saxon form of poetry. This was introduced to the children as a way of the writer helping the reader know what something looks like, smells like, or is used for – by making the words jump off the page. A pre-written kenning based on an oak tree was the starting point and the children quickly grasped the idea that they could fool their audience simply by altering the order. In this example, the first two kennings might suggest an umbrella, but the third feels like a red herring, before the fourth suggests something to do with nature. The fifth and final kenning confirms that it is indeed a tree.

Wind-protector

Shade giver

Life-provider

Squirrel's playground

Forest giant

The older children grasped the idea but those in Year 2 needed a little more help to visualise and explain their chosen object. In order to support this process, two packs of photographs of items found in the natural environment were provided: a cluster of banded snails on a wet day, a full arch rainbow, a pod of dolphins cresting on a wave, and a lighthouse sending out luminous signals. The children chose a photograph and used this as their stimulus; they also kept it hidden from the other children. When it was time to share writing through the Writers' Chair, all of the photographs were laid out on the hall floor. As the writer shared their kenning, the children had to locate the photograph on which they thought the kenning was based. This proved to be immensely popular: the aural and visual element combined with the children listening and selecting the possible choices.

The final session

The final element in any Writers' Workshop is to publish the writing, and through the process of re-crafting and refinement, the polished piece demands an audience. The final session of the six weeks was an informal book reading for parents, which gave the children the opportunity to share their writing, just as real authors do. The aim was not to present a polished assembly-like event but to share snippets, ideas and some final pieces. In order to really feel like a writer, the children had also made their own books that featured their favourite writing. Much of this writing was done at home and the children got to choose which pens or pencils to use as well as deciding on the design elements, such as how much text to put on a page and whether to include pictures.

The informality worked well, as it allowed the children to stumble and re-read without feeling they'd got anything wrong. There was an enormous sense of pride in the room from both the adults and children. The Headteacher was quick to reflect on the way in which the workshops had given a voice to the children to express their ideas through their real or imagined writings. The final writing shared on the day was from Abi, in Year 6:

Imagine a day

Where nothing turns to everything.

The impossible becomes possible.

Life never ends

And the world is heaven.

Imagine a day

Where a rollercoaster is all you know

Flowing up and down every day.

Emotions rising all around you,

Not knowing where you are.

Imagine a day

Where your hopes and dreams are in shouting distance.

Every day one wish comes true

And life is as you dream.

Figure 11.2 Rollercoaster

Conclusion

At the end of the six weeks, the children were able to express what the writing meant to them, and what they felt they had found out about themselves as developing writers. A message shared with the Headteacher prior to the project was what Christie (2003) refers to as: *Learning to write means learning to represent aspects of their world* (p.288). The children's views reflected this. Abi found writing gave her space to think about her life and to make sense of things, whereas Emily in Year 2 just liked words. Shay, in Year 4 chose to come along even though he did not seem keen on writing in class. He had two reasons: one was that he did enjoy writing; two, other children went to sports clubs and he wanted a club of his own. The Headteacher said of Shay: *He felt that he couldn't and shouldn't, and now feels he can and he will.*

Given the space and time, the children were able to write for pleasure, in much the same way that we talk about reading for pleasure. The children enjoyed the ownership over their own writing, by choosing the topic, or applying a newly-learned technique and by putting all of this into practice, the children were able to evolve as confident and creative writers.

Look for opportunities in your own classrooms to integrate a Writers' Workshop into writing lessons, or run a writing club after school or at lunchtime. Let the project's success speak for itself, and let the children guide you.

References

Children's books

Thomson, S and Gonsalves, R (2005) *Imagine a Day*. New York, US: Atheneum Press.

McMillan, I (2001) 'Ten Things Found in a Shipwrecked Sailor's Pocket' in *The Very Best of Ian MacMillan*. London: Macmillan Children's Books.

Walliams, D (2010) *Mr Stink*. London: Harper Collins Children's Books.

General

Bearne, E (2002) *Making Progress in Writing*. London: RoutledgeFalmer.

Chamberlain, L (2014) Imagine a Day When you can Ride on a Dragon and Touch a Cloud with the Tip of your Finger. Rediscovering Writers Workshop', *English 4-11*, Summer, 2014.

Christie, F (2003) Writing the World in Hall, N, Larson, J and Marsh, J (eds.) *Handbook of Early Childhood Literacy*. London: SAGE.

Clark, C (2015) *Young People's Attitudes Towards Writing, Their Writing Enjoyment and Their Writing Behaviour*. London: NLT.

Graves, DH (1983) *Writing: Teachers & Children at Work*. London: Heinemann Educational Books.

McCormick Calkins, L (1994) *The Art of Teaching Writing*. Portsmouth, NH: Heinemann.

12 Writing beyond the classroom

Writing for real purposes

The development of children's writing lives – beyond the classroom and into the home – is a way of encouraging them to see that writing is not just for school. In the introduction to this book we suggested that children should be encouraged to develop mastery over their writing through the creation of backpacks of practice. As teachers, it is important to remember that there is a writing life beyond the classroom – and the focus should be on encouraging children to bring in their backpacks of practice and letting them choose which skills or previous experiences are most useful for their school-based task. Throughout, the book has highlighted the importance of these out-of-school writing lives and the importance of meaningful writing tasks. This chapter focuses on projects that may provide a potential bridge between home and school.

There are a number of routes into writing in the home, some covert and some obvious.

- List writing can engage children in writing for a real purpose.

  o As mum or dad stand at the cupboards checking what there is and what is required, the child can be the one writing the grocery list.

  o Sorting out the chest of drawers in the bedroom can include labelling the drawers of what is to be found inside. The same idea could be extended to toy cupboards, book shelves or plastic boxes of construction toys.

- Thank you letters after birthdays or Christmas provide real letter-writing opportunities, as can sending a postcard to grandma on a day trip or a weekend away.

- A chalk board in the kitchen can be a great way to leave notes for each other.

- Writing down today's tea menu can serve two functions: it encourages the child to read what they'll be eating (but it also helps those who have school dinners and have to quickly interpret words and pictures first thing in the morning in a busy school playground).

- Filling in the family calendar with events and asking the children to contribute with either images or writing.

Although these suggestions appear to be print based, they can also involve technology through the use of *Touchnote* postcards or family organisers such as *Cozi*.

Bridging the gap

Whether children are at the mark-making stage of their development or more accomplished writers, it is important to share the outcomes of their work by displaying it on the wall, in shared areas or by publishing their work in class books or via the school website or blog. This takes the in-school writing into the community, as parents are exposed to successful writing and visitors notice that writing has a visible presence in school. These display strategies can also extend to celebrating writing completed out of school and if children find that their writing artefacts or souvenirs are welcomed, they are more likely to realise that writing can go beyond the classroom walls. It should be easy to find a space for a writing board in the classroom that children add to by pinning up writing brought in from home. It also provides a useful purpose in highlighting for you the kinds of writing that children enjoy at home. You may find that an apparently reluctant writer produces stories on the computer because they have the time and space to complete it – something that is not always possible in busy classrooms.

A feature of any Key Stage 1 classroom is the role-play area, a place where all children are encouraged to see themselves as writers by providing an environment that celebrates writing. Within a typical role-play area, there are opportunities for literate role-play activities for example, a Mrs Wobble the Waitress Restaurant with order forms, menus and notes for customer complaints. Role-play areas were based on home corners which have been a popular feature within Nursery and Reception classrooms for decades. The home corner was originally conceptualised as the place within school that provides a bridge between home experiences and the new environment called the classroom. While role-play areas have developed in sophistication and have moved into Key Stage 2 classrooms – with ideas such as the Cabinet War Rooms, the officer's quarters of the Captain of the Titanic or the flight deck of Apollo 13 – their original role was to bridge the gap between home and school.

The remainder of this chapter introduces you to three key projects which bridge the home/ school divide and encourage children, and their writing, to move freely across the gap as confident and engaged young writers.

Storysack

 Neil Griffiths devised the idea of a *Storysack*, which is an easy way of taking a story into the home and encourages a love of writing through the promotion of in-context writing activities. Within each bag (often decorated with images from the story, or in the shape of something to do with the story) there is a copy of the text for the child, along with accompanying items associated with the story: a big book; a DVD of the story or link to an e-book; related non-fiction books; props to match the key elements of the story and any activities related to the story. In order to encourage writing, there might be pens or paper, crayons or notepads. For example, in a Goldilocks Storysack, there might be three cushions – to represent the three beds – a bowl and spoon, a recipe for making porridge, and question or prompt cards to support adults in promoting language opportunities.

Being able to relive a favourite book with a Storysack enables children to bring the story to life for themselves. In the retelling for ourselves, we have the opportunity to write our own version or to rewrite or adapt the story. For example, use questions at key stages in the story: What might Flat Stanley's next adventure be? What else might the Hungry Caterpillar have eaten? A storysack can also include a copy of the text written in dual language, which can work as consolidation or pre-teaching for children for whom English is an additional language. This inclusive approach allows all parents and carers to become involved – in a playful way – with their children's reading and writing.

The sack can also provide scaffolds or prompts to promote writing. For example, these could be in the form of storyboards for the children to summarise the book, or notelets to write to their teacher saying what they think about the book. It might be they want to write a letter to a character and use a blank postcard from the sack or to make their own book, having been inspired by what they have read. In this way, parents are supported and can encourage their children with both their reading and writing. While the children enjoy a favourite story at home which they first shared at school, writing and reading become meaningful and associated with a shared experience that just so happens to have taken place across two different locations.

Curiosity kits

 Curiosity kits are book bags containing non-fiction books, along with related artefacts and activities. Just in the same way that storysacks are taken home from school, the curiosity kits also cross the home/school divide and can be easily adopted within a home reading scheme. The original project was designed as a small pilot project within the National Year of Reading in 1999 and involved whole class sets of kits being used in four different Year 4 classrooms around the country (Lewis *et al.*, 1999). The aim was to encourage and engage reluctant readers, particularly boys.

The ingredients of a curiosity kit include: a non-fiction text, related objects or items, a magazine, comment stickers or sticky notes for annotating the text, and a notebook for comments or messages. Again, the exterior of the kit is important and is related to the topic in a way that engages readers more readily than through the front cover of a print-based book. For example, a kit based *Ultimate Spy: Inside the secret world of espionage* by H. Keith Melton might be housed in an unassuming briefcase but filled with flaps and hidden pockets; a cover of a recent James Bond DVD; a magnifying glass; a James Bond magazine (carefully edited); fictitious passports; keys to an unspecified car. The possibilities are endless but potential writing activities should be at the forefront of any design. For example, the kit could include a copy of *Stormbreaker* by Anthony Horowitz with comment stickers to add to favourite sections. Children could design a new-style magazine; invent new characters or write missing scenes; devise persuasive posters; script a documentary about the secrets of James Bond's early life, or create a new Bond-style car, with endless attachments or inventions. Involve the children and ask them for ideas and thoughts, and if at this very moment you're running off to design your own kit, you know it will work for the children in your class.

Storyboxes

The idea of Key Stage 2 children enjoying and engaging with role play has long been a discussion point in staff rooms. While the idea of a traditional role-play area is not always possible because of space issues, Helen Bromley's development of *Storyboxes* overcomes this obstacle and provides yet another way of engaging children in play that can cross home and school.

Bromley's idea of *Storyboxes* is that within a simple shoebox children can enter an imagined world of Ancient Egypt, travel on a pirate ship or even learn more about the experience of a Second World War evacuee. By using artefacts included in the box, children can engage in high-level discussion and collaborative talk where they are genuinely responding to a shared

Figure 12.1 Storyboxes

experience, something on which quality writing can be based. Imagine the writing that would follow from exploring the following:

> *Evacuee's Storybox*
>
> A ration book, a letter from a grieving mother, a watch, a train ticket, a medal, a torn family photograph.
>
> *Alex Rider's Storybox*
>
> A stopwatch, torch, a fading photograph of his parents, carabiner, rope, invisible ink, mobile phone, envelope with coded letter.

Rather than you, as the teacher, deciding on the genre, allow children the opportunity to choose how they would like to respond, through poetry, a diary entry, a historically accurate report, or through an exciting narrative. Cremin *et al.* (2006) argue that teachers should refrain from determining the genre and allow children to 'seize the moment' to write. Their research suggests that when children do take ownership of the writing, the quality improves. This is especially true of writing that can be completed at home, as children will choose what feels right, or what their friend wants to write, or there may be a collaborative piece between siblings as they create maps or their own games based on their experience of the box.

While the primary objective for all three projects are related to reading, the option to develop writing is clear as a natural extension – and within a purposeful and motivational context.

References

Children's books

Stormbreaker, Anthony Horowitz. Walker Books (2015)

Ultimate Spy: Inside the secret world of espionage, H. Keith Melton. DK Children (2015).

General

Bromley, H (2002) *50 Exciting Ideas for Storyboxes*. Cambridge: Lawrence Education Publishing.

Cremin, T, Goouch, K, Blakemore, L, Goff, E and Macdonald, R (2006) Connecting Drama and Writing: Seizing the Moment to Write, *Research in Drama Education*, 11(3): 273–291

Lewis, M, Fisher, R, Grainger, T, Harrison, C and Hulme, P (1999) *Curiosity Kits: The Impact of Non-Fiction Book Bags on Boys' Reading at Home.*. Leicester: UKLA.

Storysack

www.storysack.com/

Final thoughts

Throughout this book you have been encouraged to think about writing: to think about its purpose, its audience, its context and its relevance to the lives of the children in your classes. You have been asked to think about what writing is: how you as the teacher define it, and how you share that definition with your children. You can question whether the importance of writing is based on transcription, rather than as a meaningful opportunity to be creative with language play, and to enjoy both the crafting and re-shaping of ideas. You have been challenged to make writing visible, through the way you shape your classroom environment, the value you place on writing through displays of all kinds of writing, and through the accessibility children have to appropriate writing tools within your classroom. You are asked to be the role model, to be the champion for writing as a creative act, whatever its genre. Children should see you as the facilitator rather than the expert. You should write, and write frequently, and write visibly in front of your classes. You have been set the mission to get involved, to know children's authors, to read quality children's literature, to book shadow through competitions such as the Blue Peter Book Awards or the UKLA Book Awards, which are the only awards voted on by teachers for teachers.

Most of all you have been asked to make writing something that you will think about beyond end of key stage expectations and performance descriptors. Make the most of a national curriculum that requires throughout their primary learning that *pupils should continue to have opportunities to write for a range of real purposes and audiences*. Embrace that statement and think of all the creative and enjoyable ways you can to hook children into writing – and for them to know about purpose and different audiences as part of their broad repertoire of being engaged and enthusiastic young writers.

Index